Bio-Typing
Beyond Body Language

Bio-Typing
Beyond Body Language

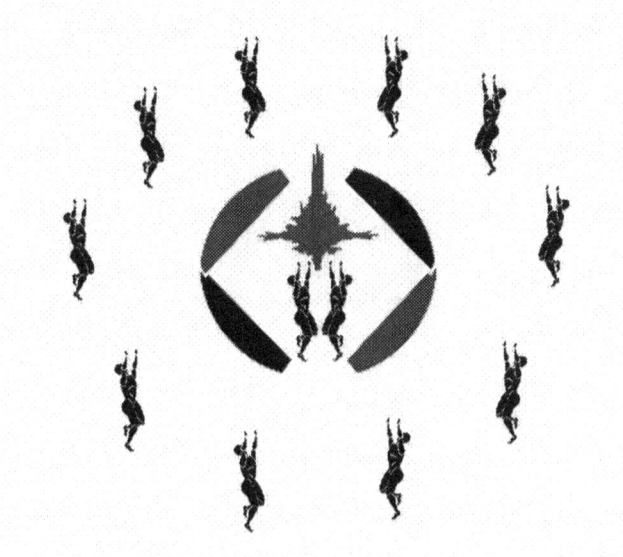

Johnny Seitz

iUniverse, Inc.
New York Lincoln Shanghai

Bio-Typing Beyond Body Language

iUniverse, Inc.

For information address:
iUniverse, Inc.
2021 Pine Lake Road, Suite 100
Lincoln, NE 68512
www.iuniverse.com

ISBN: 0-595-31677-8 (pbk)
ISBN: 0-595-66367-2 (cloth)

Printed in the United States of America

Contents

List of Illustrations

Acknowledgments

This book is dedicated to my loving wife, Chris. Without her endurance and encouragement, I would have never attained this accomplishment, gaining the privilege of sharing my life's work with you, the reader.

There are many people in my life to whom I would like to express sincere gratitude in supporting me through the process of creating this book.

One very special person, Sindi (Rust) Westberg, stands out in my mind and heart. In the mid-1990s, my wife and I moved to Ecuador, South America because of our love and commitment to the rain forest and its people. We formed an ecotourism company and took people deep into the Amazon rainforest. This is how we met Sindi, who had heard about my work in America and wanted to experience it herself. What she discovered made a profound impact on her. As an educator fresh out of Harvard, she felt that many people could benefit from the Bio-Typing information. I will never forget her telling me, "Come on, you can't retire into to the jungles of South America and not share this. It will change people's lives!" Sindi, God bless her, became the catalyst and partner for getting this material out.

I would like to acknowledge two other key people. My colleague Sebastian Gendry was principal in my writing process, and Laurel Fishman offered her priceless editorial contributions and grace under pressure. Both have shared an absolute commitment to the successful completion of this project!

There is also my dear friend Liane Holliday-Willey, who has shown me that there are many, many other people who, like me, have autism and also have much to offer the world.

I am grateful to all of those I have worked with over the course of my life that have inspired the creation of my system of Bio-Typing. I give my special love and thanks to my compassionate mother in-law, Suzy Gallo; my teachers Marcel Marceau and Etienne Decroux; and everyone else who has supported me over the years: Veronica Uribe, Lisa Edelstein, Randy Smith, Kate McHale, Coco Maldonado, Adam Sheck, Doctors Kevin and Sai Ling Michaels, John Westberg, Archie Chechoo, Bebop, Diane Bohem, Eugene Reddest, Grandfather Albert Ward, Granny Wolf, Anne Snyder, Heather Larkin, Judy Andersen, Keith Patchel, Marion Leone, Samuel Claiborne, Pedro and Irina Saad, Tim Kelley and Wayne Tobias.

Foreword

◆

An Incredible Gift

By Liane Holliday Willey, Ed.D.

As an adult with autism, Johnny Seitz lives in a very different place than the people around him. The autistic mind tends toward detail and mental pictures, and as such, it is very focused and free of many of the expected preconceptions that can limit the neurotypical (so-called "normal") mind from unbiased observation. This quality can allow the autistic person to see details and subtle interactions in an incredibly complex system. This is bound to produce new discoveries. Many of these, I believe, will ultimately revolutionize the rest of the world's perception of things. What an incredible gift, and my friend Johnny Seitz has it.

History provides us with examples of many scholars who had this gift. Leonardo da Vinci was able to see and understand the human body with a depth and accuracy that was unequaled in his day. Albert Einstein saw the true nature of the universe and was remarkably able to distill that realization down to a four-letter explanation of the interactions of atomic nature, one that literally changed science's understanding of reality: $e=mc^2$.

While no one knows for certain if da Vinci or Einstein had a form of autism or not, many top researchers in the field now believe these geniuses at least had a number of traits consistent with autism. Like many super-bright people with autism, they had the kind of mind that is capable of taking a profoundly complex system and not only understanding it, but also appreciating its potential and expressing it in practical terms.

Beyond history, one has to look no further than today's Silicon Valley and its reported unusually large community of people with autism. They are living examples of the unique mindset that is so extraordinarily capable of understanding and creating the computer codes we all use but cannot even begin to comprehend.

It is Johnny's own particular gift that allows him to perceive and understand very complex systems of physical movement. His gift also enables him to systemize, and ultimately apply, his analyses to the human body.

Like so many young children with autism, Johnny was unable to accurately interpret the communications of most of the other people around him. Experts refer to this inability as "mind blindness." In short, Johnny could not "read" the people around him. He could not tell if they were teasing him or welcoming him, feeling angry, happy or annoyed with him—even if they were aware of him at all. Incredibly, Johnny was innately able to develop a technique of observation and an applied interactional methodology that allowed him to better read the people in his world.

In an organic and natural way, Johnny taught himself how to read people's subtle body movements—their body's physics, if you will. This ability has served Johnny well from childhood and has taken him to great success. He has worked as a teacher at the university level, a mime in several countries, and most recently as a life coach/therapist in Los Angeles. In this capacity, he is much sought-after for his ability to help others understand the deeply rooted and usually subconscious truth and reasons behind their responses to situations and interactions with people. I am not at all certain how he does it, but trust me, he does. I have seen him do it.

After just a short time spent observing my three children, my husband and I in the first moments he met us, Johnny was uncannily accurate in his ability to describe our basic personality types.

While most people do not have the mind blindness of a person with autism, there are few who would not admit to being confused by other's actions or reactions to many situations. Think about a job interview, meeting strangers or socializing with your partner's co-workers, and you will probably remember times when you were perplexed and unsure about how to figure out and relate to a particular person. Put another way, you were unable to break that person's personality code. With Johnny's system as your guide, you will be able to break that code and make valid predictions about another person's general personality type. You will even discover the way people assimilate and process information.

Johnny has taught his system to hundreds of people who use it in their own lives, and its endless possibilities are just beginning to be realized. Here's hoping you will take Johnny's insight and make it your own!

—Liane Holliday Willey, Ed.D. is the author of Pretending to be Normal: Living With Asperger's Syndrome, Asperger's Syndrome in the Family: Redefining Normal and Asperger's Syndrome in Adolescence: Living With the Ups, the Downs and Things in Between.

Preface

✦

Where It All Began

I live in a world that is parallel to yours and yet separate from yours.
We share the air we both breathe.
We share the stars we both walk under.
I do not share your understanding of people's minds,
Nor can you share the silent joys or the terrors that I know.

I am battered by forces that you cannot see or hear.
I am constantly shaken to my roots by winds you cannot feel.
Things that you don't even notice overwhelm me constantly,
And I get totally lost in fascination with things you never see,
And often I completely miss your smiles and your frowns.

My memories are often hidden from me,
Like a handful of marbles spread across a parking lot.
My emotions sometimes leap upon me from out of nowhere,
And I often can't remember the simplest things, like how to get home,
And I remember the most obscure, like serial numbers and license plates.

I walk in ways that you sometimes find funny.
I forget faces, and I am embarrassed when I do not know who you are.
I sometimes need to flap my hands or sway my body to find where I left it.
I need to control as many things as I can to make my world as safe as possible.
I am a child you cannot see, in the body of an adult you don't understand.

© Johnny Seitz 2000

This book tells how a person who had a very different perspective on the world learned to read and understand the other people in his world in order to interact with them more effectively.

Hi, my name is Johnny Seitz. I was born with high—functioning autism, also known as Asperger's Syndrome. Currently, there is an ongoing dialogue on the differences between Asperger's Syndrome and classical autism. Some argue that both are on the same spectrum. From 2000 to 2004, the surge in media focus on Asperger's Syndrome and autism allowed anyone to pick up a magazine almost monthly and find an article on the subject. There has been significant television coverage, including on *60 Minutes*, and there is ample material about Asperger's Syndrome and autism on the Internet. All of these mediums have given the public plenty of information to join the discussion regarding the differences.

Figure 1: Johnny Seitz at age 17

Autism gave me a radically different perspective on life than that of other people. Most children share a common context with other people; they know how others think, based on how they themselves think. This allows them to know a lot about how other people will process and respond to what they say or do, because they take in things in the same way themselves. I, however, had to learn to work my way into the psyches of other people from the outside, in order to understand what they were saying and to be able to communicate with them at all.

There seems to be wealth of information that everyone else automatically understands about social interactions that people with autism just sort of miss. My friend Liane says people with autism take everything literally. I know that when some guy would say, "Hey there, Johnny, what's the good word?" I would really try hard to guess, quite literally, what the good word was. Liane says there are just a lot of things that normal children understand about human interaction by osmosis that we with autism miss. Adults, Liane says, tell children to look others in the eye when they talk to you, but no one needs to tell them this is something a boy does not do in the boys' locker-room shower after gym class.

I would look at people and think I understood what they were thinking and feeling. Yet when I approached them and tried to interact with them based on what I had understood, things would begin to go downhill fast! Most of what I perceived about people was in stark contradiction to what they told me they were actually thinking and feeling. I got strong impressions about them, but the people involved often totally denied that the impressions I got were correct.

Part of this misunderstanding was my fault, because they thought in ways entirely different from the way that I thought. Part of the fault was theirs, because they just didn't want to admit to the feelings I perceived they had. In some ways, I am like a dog that understands when you are upset and responds accordingly, only to have you ask me why I am acting so weird around you. Your anger is something inside of you, but I feel it and I react to it, even if it is not an overt, or obvious, part of your interaction with me.

This apparently unresolved contradiction caused me to develop a total absorption and fascination with the possible meanings of people's body language. The bottom line was I never knew what response I was going to get when I approached and spoke to strangers, or even with people I already knew.

What I Learned From All of This

If you, like me, have ever tried to share an important idea with someone else and failed miserably by using the wrong approach; and were left feeling that the rug had been pulled from under your feet. Perhaps you have tried to get to know a stranger; initiate a friendship or start a relationship and failed miserably; or you have had the experience of your spouse or your friend simply not comprehending what you were saying; then you know exactly what I am talking about.

Well, I figured it out. I had to, because if I were ever going to communicate with people, I was going to have to figure out who they really were, not just what they wanted me to see when I looked at them.

In this book, I would like to share with you how I learned to understand and to interact successfully with all the different types of people in my world, a way that can bring you the same successful outcomes.

Your Words Say Little. Your Body Says a Lot.

We are all aware of the ways that we, as humans, show ourselves and our fears and desires to one another through our nonverbal communication, but we still primarily rely upon a person's verbal communication to determine another's personality.

In fact, the average person really looks only at another person's face and the clothing he is wearing to form an evaluation. A facial expression may tell us the emotion of the moment, and clothing may be an indicator of professional or social status. Underneath all this lies a far more profound world of things to be gleaned—if you know what to look for.

The spoken word has become all-powerful. Yet it is recognized commonly by communication specialists that about 70 percent of any communication is the nonverbal part! People speak more and more, and yet they may communicate less and less. Words can be misleading and misinterpreted. There is what is thought, what is said and how it is said. This is then filtered by what the listener wants to hear, what he actually hears and what he understands of what is said. This is getting complicated! The more people learn to speak and listen, the more they forget to look at each other, closing their eyes to most of the real message. The human body never lies. It is a perfect mirror of the real you, 24 hours a day, seven days a week.

To survive, I created a way of seeing people and categorizing them into specific groups with specific rules for handling each of them, a way that works every time!

To give you an example, my friend Sebastian once introduced me to someone he knew well and asked me what I saw when I looked at that person. I told Sebastian I was seeing a man that was independent by nature, logical in his approach to things and process-oriented. I also said Sebastian's friend would wait to let another say whatever this other person was thinking before Sebastian's friend would put forth his own feelings. And I saw in Sebastian's friend a person that would collect information about other people or situations until he had enough data to decide how he would fit with them. In Sebastian's friend, I could also see a person that would test other people's ideas or recommendations before subscribing to them, even if those other people were recognized authorities. After I told Sebastian all I saw in his friend, he said the assessment was completely accurate.

The Art and Science of Really Seeing People

There is a secret language behind human movements. We have all learned to read body language in situations of physical intimacy. When we are with a loved one, we can easily see the relaxed muscles and openness of limbs that invite physical approach. We can all also see the tension of the muscles and closed limbs that forbid approach. This is just the tip of the iceberg, yet we rarely look beyond it. In everyday life we listen closely to other people's words, but we tend to ignore the body. We do this even more so if that body is under a business suit or an official uniform.

Yet underneath the complex outer surface of gender, age, facial expression, clothing or various types of uniforms, there exists a far more profound (yet simple) world of things to be read—if you know what to look for. I am not referring to what is commonly understood as "body language": looking at a person's actions and analyzing what they mean. While this serves some purpose, we are not really going to learn to understand each other much better through reference books and lists of body-language messages to be read.

My alternative way of looking at each other and ourselves is simple. It reveals the essence of people, what their main personality strengths and weaknesses are, how they make decisions and much more. You can access these insights anytime, anywhere. In all likelihood, this system is unlike anything you have ever seen before.

A Practical Application in My Own Life

Here is an example in which being able to Bio-Type someone helped to facilitate conflict resolution. In 1998, my wife and I were in the middle of a potentially dangerous situation in the jungle. We were trying to defuse an imminent confrontation between radical members of the tribe with whom we were working in Ecuador and oil company representatives. It seems the oil company had promised the tribe motors for their canoes. When the promise was not fulfilled, some of the more radical members of the tribe decided to hold a few of the oil company trucks as ransom for the undelivered motors.

My wife and I found ourselves held captive inside the oil compound, seeking to negotiate a settlement to prevent a physical confrontation. The head representative of the oil company with whom we had to deal with was standing with his widely spread feet firmly planted, unwilling to listen to anyone. He insisted things would go his way or not at all!

Figure 2: The head executive of the oil company we had to deal with was standing firmly planted over widely spread feet, not listening to us at all.

I recalled the lessons I had learned the hard way as a child when confronted by someone who stood in the same way the oil company rep was standing. I remembered calling these people "Pyramid People" because they stood so firmly planted on the ground and were so steadfast in their perspective. I had learned that a person who stands firmly rooted over a wide base of support is expecting opposition. To me, this type of person seemed to feel challenged, and thus, he felt the need to prove something—or at least prove he could hold his ground. Pyramid People also had an exasperating tendency to repeat themselves over and over again.

So this confrontation between the tribe and the oil company was nothing new for me, and I could see hope in the situation. I motioned to my wife to look at the oilman's feet and stood the same way, rooting myself to the earth. I had told her about the lessons I learned the hard way as a child when I was confronted with people who stood in this way. Pyramid People, whom I would later Bio-Type as Torso-Sway Walkers, required special handling if I were to get through to them. Since it seemed they felt the need to prove something, I had learned never to oppose them head-on. They would not back down easily from a position they took or a goal they were intent on achieving.

Though they had appeared strongly rooted into their ideas, I had also learned they were open to other ways of thinking. When they would make a shift, they would do so in a major way, moving their entire base of thoughts, opinions and emotions together with their body. I had discovered that the best way to deal with them was to let them do a lot of talking before I even thought to open my mouth.

I learned to let them lay out their whole presentation, which usually included much of their own philosophical viewpoints. To establish rapport, I learned to listen with an open mind; careful not to respond with anything that might indicate an opposing point of view. My response would then carefully include their perspective, paralleled with my viewpoint, so that they could see my point as part of their own viewpoint—or at least something corresponding to it. I would preface what I needed to say with something like, "Yes, and you know how you said you believed such-and-such? Well, what I was thinking was kind of the same thing, actually. You see…"

We had never met before, but I already knew exactly how to deal with the oil rep. We began coaxing a detailed explanation out of him, how he saw the situation and how he thought it should be handled. We patiently waited for him to finish his lengthy explanation, and then we were able to bridge his values with what we thought might work to settle the issue at hand, using the same methods I had learned as a child.

The oil rep felt he resolved the conflict with his own ingenuity, thus keeping his authority intact in front of the tribe. No matter what his perspective was, the outcome worked! With the knowledge of his Bio-Type, Torso-Sway Walker, we were able to achieve effective communication in an intimidating situation. If we had been opposed to hearing him out and not empathized with his point of view, we wouldn't have attained the positive resolution.

My Method of Dealing with People Explained

Humans do things differently from one another; this much can't be argued. While countless expressions of our personalities do exist, there are only so many muscles available for any given task. Which muscles a person uses can be very telling. Knowing what to look for will show you how to read people.

This crucial observation is the key I use to read people with remarkable accuracy. While the outcome may sometimes seem magical, but there is really no magic in it at all. The "muscle methodology," which people use to hold their bodies upright and to do things physically, is exactly the same methodology they use to approach and solve problems in other areas of their lives. It is the way that a person's body learned to approach and solve physical problems as a child that is clearly written in the way they hold their body today. The way an individual approaches and solves physical problems today is the model he has applied to approaching and solving mental, emotional and interpersonal problems in the past.

What I call Bio-Typing is a method of personality analysis that goes far beyond what is conventionally called body language. Interpreting body language entails looking at people's bodily postures and gestures, then determining what these mean.

In his book *The Roots of the Self*, Robert Ornstein says, "Temperament is the basic rootstock of individuality." He theorizes about three dimensions of a person's individuality, based on the brain's orchestration of the interplay among various areas of the brain. My work shows how the body responds to the messages set forth by the brain. Each of the three Bio-Types uses a specific set of what I have termed "muscle recruitment patterns" to carry out specific actions in response to messages sent by the brain.

These muscle recruitment patterns are the result of how each child discovered ways of using his own body in early developmental stages. Developed by each child in response to his environment and relationship to his world, the child's muscle recruitment patterns are determined by the choices of muscles his body recruits for physical movements. All people's muscle recruitment patterns shape the body of the adult they eventually become.

There is no "normal" way of breathing, walking or anything else, for that matter, so there are no standard muscle recruitment patterns. In each case, the child a person once was continues to be visible in the body of the adult he is today. Much of what I refer to as "personality" is basically the result of how people approached and solved problems in every area of their life. Most of these problem-solving methodologies were first established in physical problem solving, so Bio-Typing is a look at personality in its most foundational physical aspect.

When it comes to the actual meaning of 'personality' in relation to Bio-Typing, it represents who you are in life, the way in which you respond to life and all of the diverse coping mechanisms that have walked you through life. I base my work on the mind-body connection that tells us about the physical manifestations of how we initially approached and solved problems physically.

According to Arthur Reber in the *Dictionary of Psychology*, the term *personality* is "resistant to definition and so broad in its usage that no coherent simple statement about it can be made…The most complete typological theory was that of W.H. Sheldon, who elegantly (but unconvincingly) argued that body types are intimately related to personality development."

Personality type theories date back to Hippocrates, who hypothesized about four basic temperaments of personality. Arthur Reber outlines eight of the more "influential, general orientations." I won't bore you by talking about all eight, but I will name them, just to give you an idea of the in-depth, ongoing discussion as to the meaning of personality. Reber lists the basic personality type categories as: type theories, trait theories, psychodynamic and psychoanalytic theories, behaviorism, humanism, social learning theories, situationism and interactionism.

There are countless systems of personality assessment available in the world today. I have broadly grouped them into three categories.

Systems from the first category are based on natural cycles and how they relate to the individual. Two examples of this are represented in Chinese medicine and Astrology. All systems based on natural cycles require knowing when the particular individual was born.

Systems from the second category deal with the mind. Mostly, they are based on direct questioning. A set of determining questions is asked of an individual, and the answers he gives determine his qualifying as a predetermined personality type. Most popular in this group of systems are the Myers-Briggs Type Indicator (MBTI) and the Enneagram. These methods are powerful in identifying who a person really is. Their drawback is the complexity of their application. For example, the MBTI requires a person answer more than 300 questions before finding out his type. Some adaptations of the MBTI ask as few as 60 questions.

Systems from the third category are movement-based assessments of the body. A great deal of advanced research has been carried out in the last twenty years in nonverbal communication. Practitioners in many fields have studied just about every conceivable aspect of human behavior that relates to how people communicate. There are many different approaches, and you may have read books about some of them. Each model teaches that everything has a meaning, from the shape of your limbs to the tiniest movements of your eyes. You may even have tried to memorize lists of positions or gestures and their corresponding psychological explanation. Your challenge then becomes remembering the meanings of each characteristic.

Bio-Typing Is Different…

You do not need to talk to a person beforehand or find out information about him to know his Bio-Type. I like to say it works well, especially because you never get a second chance to make a good first impression. With Bio-Typing, you get to know almost immediately who is in front of you without having to ask his astrological sign or any of countless other personality-defining questions.

As you read this book, you will discover my perspective of not one, but three distinct patterns to human muscle recruitment. Your own body perfectly falls into one of these three patterns. Bio-Typing is about categorizing people into what I call Bio-Types. The three Bio-Types have distinctive movement patterns based on the Bio-Type's muscle recruitment pattern.

Each of the Bio-Types is grouped as such because of the similarities that all people of a given Bio-Type share in their muscle recruitment. These groupings transcend gender, age, race and culture. Surprising as it may seem, a short, squat individual and a tall, lanky one can both fit into the same Bio-Type. Whether stocky or slim, whether an elegant dresser or a football player, they can exhibit similar muscle recruitment patterns and be grouped into the same Bio-Type. Perhaps more surprisingly, each person of a specific Bio-Type approaches and deals with other people in remarkably similar fashion. In turn, any person of a specific Bio-Type can be effectively related to in specific ways.

By recognizing that people think and act differently based on their Bio-Type, you can learn to set aside your own expectations and judgments. By applying Bio-Typing, you can immediately adapt your communication style to meet any situation skillfully, as it arises. Consequently, you will relate to more people with deeper understanding and continued enjoyment of the process.

From the workplace to the home, knowing people's Bio-Type is a crucial piece of information that can be useful in almost any situation with them.

Each Bio-Type likes information delivered to him in a certain way and is better suited physically and emotionally for some approaches rather than others. Although the issues you need to work out with a spouse, a colleague or a child may be emotionally charged; knowing how the other person's Bio-Type approaches and solves problems in every area of his life is an invaluable tool in getting your point across.

I see the bodies people live in today as the result of how they saw themselves as children in relation to their world and how they faced the challenges of growing up. I believe that in many ways, people's bodies are the most tangible manifestation of how their minds actually work. I hope to demonstrate that if you really look at the manner in which people do things physically, you will find yourself looking precisely at how they approach and solve problems mentally and/or emotionally—in every area of their lives.

Apparently This Is Something New

It seems that few, if any experts have noticed these dramatic differences in the muscle recruitment patterns used by different individuals to perform the same action. Up until now, most body physiology and exercise texts have assumed that there was only one "normal" way of using the human body to perform a given task. Maybe this is because the people that initially came up with this idea used their mind to "see" other people's bodies. Growing up with autism, I had to use other people's bodies to "see" their minds.

Throughout my life, I have felt like a visitor on an alien planet where everyone else looked like me but thought and did things in ways that were very different from me. I came to understand how others did things, just not why. What follows is the set of observations and "rules of engagement" I developed as a child and young adult, ways that I devised to get by.

In my quest, I had certain advantages. I have always seen many things that most people miss. I am unable to retain an image of what a person's face looks like, but I see clearly how people hold themselves, stand and walk, and especially how they approach and interact with others. I learned to see people as the children that they once were by looking at their bodies and reading backwards.

Temple Grandin, another person with autism, refers to herself as an "anthropologist on Mars" because she had to study other people to figure out how they thought so that she could relate with them. The same thing happened to me, except that she studied their minds, while I studied their bodies.

I chose to lead my life involved in fields of either human expression or the physical mechanics of human movement. I worked as a classical ballet dancer, professional mime, choreographer and personal trainer. Thirty years of research, hands-on experience and insight led me to develop something of a topographical map of the human psyche written across the human body. Although it is a landscape we are all familiar with, I have explored and mapped this terrain as no one I know about has done before.

My Path to Successful Interpersonal Relationships

As strange as it may seem, I never thought what I discovered was any big deal. In fact, I did not even give it a name or think about sharing it with anyone else until I was well into adulthood. I had mentioned I had a system I used to read people, but only in passing to close friends and occasionally to students during seminars and classes I taught. Basically I assumed everyone else was able to know these same things about people when they looked at each other. To me, it was as clear as day, written in bold capital letters all over their bodies. It was broadcast constantly to whoever was willing to listen, or more accurately, willing to look.

As time went on, however, more and more friends, students and clients started telling me they were not seeing what I saw when I looked at people. People in my life began asking me to share with them how I managed to know so much about others just by watching them walk. Mysteriously to me, they did not see what I did, and they definitely wanted to learn more. I found myself explaining something that had become obvious to me in my process of figuring out how best to interact with the people who wandered in and out of my world.

I have found a simple path to successful interpersonal relationships. Just as knowing someone is a fire sign might give you hints about his personality, what I am about to show you will give you meaningful, specific insights about how to better understand and be understood by every person you will ever meet. You will learn how to best interact with different types of people and have successful communications.

My sincere hope is that this work serves as a bridge between individuals. Perhaps they have been in each other's lives for years and yet do not really understand one another or perhaps they are meeting each other for the first time.

As you read along, keep in mind this book is written by someone that still has trouble understanding exactly the way other people think. I sometimes get very detailed about expressing my ideas. You might find my approach a bit different from what you may be used to, so let me share with you a bit about where I am coming from.

1

I Cannot See Your Face—I Read Your Body

"They are a bright thread in the rich tapestry of life. Our civilization would be extremely dull and sterile if we did not have and treasure people with Asperger's Syndrome."

—Tony Attwood, Ph.D., The Morning News, Vol. 11, No. 3

I was diagnosed with autism as a child. The Bio-Typing system of body language analysis was born for me out of dire necessity. As a child, I started creating it intuitively to help me overcome my specific challenges. Compared to the majority of the population, you might say I am socially impaired. You see, social rules of human communication and the so-called logic of other people's thoughts and feelings are, and always have been, a mystery to me.

I recently learned a new term. It seems I am "mind-blind."

Because I lacked insight into what other people thought or how they perceived things, my childhood was challenging. I would very innocently and repeatedly do things many people did not like; behaving in ways they probably felt were sheer provocation on my part. Since I never seemed to do the right thing, social interactions were daunting. I wanted to participate as others did, but I just did not know how. Over the years, I dealt the best I could with other people's difficulties in dealing with me.

A natural performer, I could provide entertainment by imitating mannerisms and ways of walking, so people were always willing to be more patient than they might otherwise have been. If adults were not always amused by what they saw as my eccentricities or were irritated by my social gaffes, they usually forgave me in consideration of the unusual talents they saw me demonstrate. Did I mention that I am a professional mime? I have been a mime all my life. I learned to use the art of mime as a way of looking more like the people all around me, as a way to blend in. This naturally evolved into a profession as well.

My young peers were not amused. There came a time in my life when trouble was constantly around the corner. I had no idea why, and did not even suspect I was the cause of it. All I knew was that I had to find ways to avoid it. I actually fist-fought most of my way through grade school and high school.

How I learned to understand people evolved from observing and imitating others. Seeing someone walking toward me, I would instinctively match the way he was holding himself. Even if I were blind to what a person might be thinking, I was good at imitating his physical body's set of tensions and the way he moved. This led me to my first important discovery. In assuming a person's body position and moving as they moved, I felt a deep connection between intention and movement.

I might think, holding my body like this feels as if I am going to pick up something and throw it. Aha! Maybe this guy is going to pick me up and throw me! Or it might come to me, I'm standing the way he is standing, and it's the way I would stand if I would be analyzing someone in great depth. Yeah! This man is studying me. These types of observations happened repeatedly, and I rarely made wrong guesses. It became a regular occurrence. I stopped seeing limbs casually moving. Instead, I began to see the intent that was moving people.

In the mid 1980s, a new hypothesis emerged in the field of autism, termed "the theory of mind." It put forth the assumption that "normal" people have a basic, common, yet profound understanding of how each other's heads work because they share the same social upbringing. With that comes a common understanding of what you talk about and should not mention. It therefore follows that most people share an innate ability to extract certain common "rules of engagement" for social interaction.

For example, although honesty is a virtue emphasized in society, nobody needs to tell a normal child that even if Aunt Millie is obese, the child does not need to point it out to her. And that while a person should not waste his or her valuable time, walking away in the middle of a conversation that bores you is also not socially correct.

I understand some of these concepts now, but back then, I sometimes had zero finesse in interpersonal relationships. The average person picks up social graces without even realizing it, almost by osmosis. One of the most common characteristics among people with autism we are incapable of noticing social cues. This is one of the mysteries of the workings of the autistic brain. I have learned what I know about successful social interactions the hard way, through a long process of trial and error. In my case, I often felt as if I were scrutinized, put on trial and condemned.

I was a difficult child for both my relatives and the world at large: I constantly followed my own agenda. I dealt with the world from a non-neurotypical (non-"normal") viewpoint. My imagination was extremely vivid.

What I visualized often turned into what I believed. Therefore, I often acted in accordance with my perception of the world. For example, when leaving a store, I had to walk out in the exact same way I had walked in, and nobody could make me change my mind about the need to do it. I was a modern-day Theseus, and like the ancient Greek story of him in the Labyrinth, I would lay an invisible life-saving string behind me through the labyrinth-alleys of the store. The string was my map, and I needed to follow it to get back out. If I did not exit the same way I entered, the string would obviously become all tangled up with me in it, and I might be stuck in the store forever.

I do not remember being asked why I saw things like this, but it didn't matter anyway. To me, that string was real. There was no way I was going to get stuck. To this day, I still feel uncomfortable if I do not exit a store by retracing my steps. This type of ritualistic behavior is typical of persons with autism, at any age.

As if this were not enough, I also have another bizarre characteristic known as "face blindness"; the inability to register differences in human faces. I recognize and separate people based on bodily movement patterns and sometimes voice qualities, rather than facial traits. Oddly enough, identical twins do not look identical to me, not in the least bit!

There was an incident where one of my high school teachers walked up to me and started talking about a class assignment. After what seemed to be ten confused minutes, I blurted out, "Who are you, and what are you talking about?" Another time, someone I had met the night before at a party came up to me and began talking, and there I was, madly trying to figure out if I really knew her and what my relationship to her could possibly be.

I never knew or even considered that I might be the one who was different until well into my thirties. The first revelation that began to explain the puzzle of the differences between my world and that of those around me came when I took a seminar focusing on natural intuitive powers and meditation. A professor at Brooklyn College, New York, facilitated a session in which the students were hooked up to a biofeedback machine. The hook up enabled the professor and students to monitor the activity of our brainwaves while we tried to focus and reach a meditative state.

The professor informed us that the electrical activity emanating from our brain is displayed in the form of brainwaves. There are four categories of these brainwaves, ranging from those with the most activity to the least activity: Beta, Alpha, Theta and Delta. When the brain is aroused and actively engaged in mental activities, it generates Beta waves. This is where we expected to be to begin with. The next level, the Alpha state, represents non-arousal. During reflection or light meditation, a person usually generates Alpha brainwaves. Next is the Theta state. It occurs naturally in sleep and is the portion where the emotional body recuperates, heals and "tunes" itself for the next day. In the non-sleep state, Theta is associated with intense creativity, visualization ability, imagination and problem solving, and usually is present during deep meditation.

The goal of the seminar was to lead us to attain the Theta state by performing a series of suggested mental exercises. We would know when we had gotten to the Theta state by the biofeedback machine dipping into the Theta brainwave area. When my turn came, they hooked me up and waited a few moments. They then began tapping the box, checking the leads to my head, and stood there scratching their heads. The machine said I was already "naturally" in Theta. In fact, I tend to live in the Theta state. The Theta state is the "eternal now" state of consciousness. It was the Alpha and Beta states that I would need to work on. A light went on inside me. This explained a lot.

It explained why the "now" for me is the totality of my awareness. I do not relate to the notions of "earlier" and "later on." I am present in each moment, and this is all I know. In fact, if I saw you last ten years ago, it feels exactly like last week to me.

I had made an important discovery about myself, and there was still more to come in the revelations department.

Asperger's Syndrome

I first heard the word "autism" in my childhood, in explanation of some of my unusual behaviors. Back then, though, it did not really quite fit. To have autism meant, "You don't talk, and you are mentally deficient." I was neither. The answer came much later. When I was entering my forties, a friend gave me a book that opened my eyes. In reading the book, I discovered that I experience a form of autism called Asperger's Syndrome.

Generally, when someone thinks of autism, he thinks about the title character portrayed by Dustin Hoffman in the film Rain Man. Hoffman's character was lost in a world of his own, totally disconnected from the rest of humanity. He was a person with "low-functioning autism." (Incidentally, Gerry Newport, the man Dustin Hoffman studied to develop his character in the movie, is a friend of mine. He does not have the mental retardation the Hoffman film character portrayed.)

There is another form of autism referred to as "high-functioning autism," or Asperger's Syndrome. Surprisingly enough, this condition is quite common. Often people will have a relative who is considered gifted, but eccentric. These eccentricities are often part of a much larger pattern that may well qualify as Asperger's Syndrome.

One time, for some reason I will never understand, my parents sent me to sleepover camp. This was not a good idea! At night, lying in a strange bed amid bunches of strangers; I did what I always did when I was upset. I began banging my head against the metal headboard of the bed in the large common sleeping room. I was aware that the others began talking about me, but the only way I could deal with all of the new and strange sensations of this sleepover camp was by pounding my head. Thus, I did. For someone with autism, rocking and head-banging are excellent methods of containment.

For me, autism has been both a curse and a blessing. The curse destined me never to be fully "with it," yet never fully "without it," either. I saw so much more than others did when I looked at people. I just did not always understand why it meant what I felt it meant. This created conflict and tension in many situations. For example, I would sometimes know when certain people were angry with me or attracted to me, but they refused to admit it. I deeply knew I was right, yet I had no rational proof to validate it to myself, let alone anyone else. Was this all born of my own fantasy? Was I mad? Yet it always turned out that I had been right in these cases. So how could I know things that the person himself did not seem to know?

There was only one way to find out. I made up my mind to conduct empirical research and back up my intuitions scientifically. My intention was to prove my theory that people's bodies were really telling me what I felt they were telling me by finding exactly what it was that I was seeing, that there were indeed measurable things that I was looking at, and that if others knew where to look, they would see the same things I did. This set me on a path of close physical observation, a path I have never left.

In time, I discovered that I was endowed with all the qualities I needed to overcome every single challenge I would ever have to face. I do not think I could ask for more, and I would not trade the way I am for any other way of being.

People with different forms of autism often have obsessions. Mine had always been to understand the mechanics of the human body. My special gift is the ability to encompass such a multifaceted system as the human body and to picture it easily, all at once, in all of its apparent complexity.

I am a natural mime, and when I watch someone doing something, I can actually feel the internal mechanics of this person's body. I really know what his muscles must be doing in order for him to move the way he does. By choosing to "become" him, I can feel his feelings.

Study in Europe

After graduating from high school in 1967, I enrolled at Marquette University in Milwaukee and signed up for an introductory mime class a part of my studies. Because I had always excelled at imitating normal people, I also excelled in that class. In fact, I was so good at being able to imitate the way people moved that the following year I was recruited to help teach the class. The field of human expression through movement always fascinated me. At this point, I yearned to become a professional ballet dancer. When I received a scholarship to study ballet at the Stephen Wenta Academy in Los Angeles, I left Marquette University.

Figure 3: Marcel Marceau and Johnny Seitz backstage in New York.

One evening, I snuck backstage to see a show by world-renowned mime Marcel Marceau in Los Angeles. While lurking around backstage, I got caught and was being thrown out of the theatre when Marceau walked by asking if anyone had change for the soda machine. Grabbing the opportunity, I dug into my pocket and threw a handful of coins in front of him on the floor. He told the security guards to let me go, and I became his guest for the evening. We became fast friends, and one month later, I moved to Paris at his invitation to study at his academy. I later went on to study with Marceau's own teacher, Etienne Decroux, the father of modern mime.

In class one day, Decroux brought me to a turning point in my life. Listening to him speak to the class, I found myself puzzled by Decroux's remark that humanity walked in one of three ways. He described these ways of walking as the "Push Walk," the "Pull Walk" and the "Fall Walk." His observations planted a seed in my head, an idea that was to become the foundation of Bio-Typing.

I came to see for myself that people really do walk in one of three very specific ways. However, while Decroux looked at how to use his observations to generate dramatic content when he saw "push," "pull" and "fall" movements, I was looking at muscle mechanics. This was the start of my discovery that the muscle recruitment patterns used to engage in walking are a doorway into personality.

As Desmond Morris says in *Man Watching: a Field Guide to Human Behavior*, "The Walk is an action we all take so much for granted and yet, when analyzed as a mechanical operation, it emerges as an immensely complex process—so complicated, in fact, that muscle experts are still arguing today over the finer points of how it operates…The act of walking, apart from its role in body health, is vitally important in providing a form of progression that operates as an integral part of an environment-checking and assessing system." See for yourself! Look at people walking by. People walk in many different ways. How many different ways can you see?

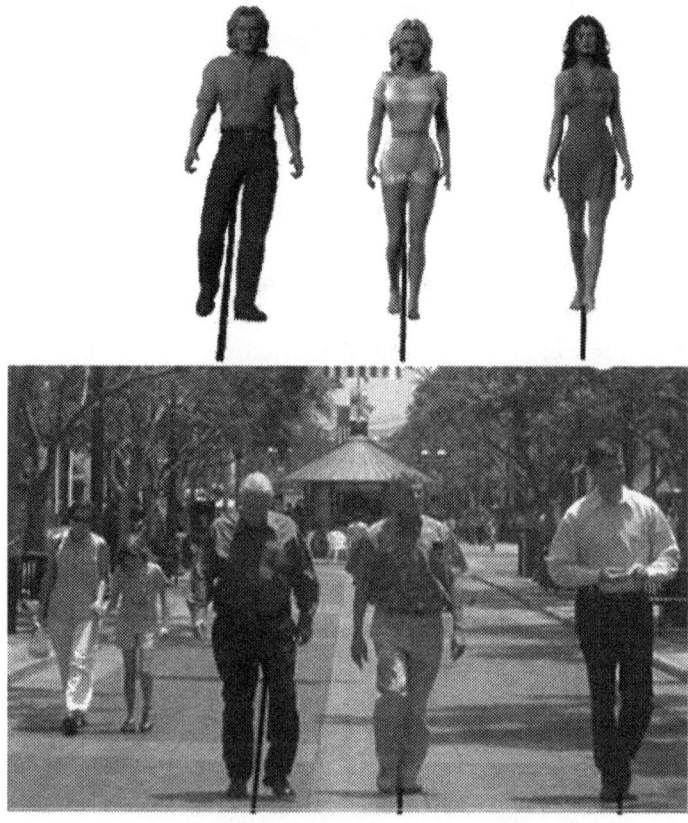

Figure 4: It's easier at the beginning to just observe the distance between people's feet as they walk

I agree with Decroux that there are three different ways to walk, but I see them a bit differently. Some people swing from side to side (figure 4, left). Some pull themselves forward using the muscles in the back of their thighs (figure 4, center). The rest are constantly pushing off with the ball of the trailing foot and falling forward onto the leading foot (figure 4, right). At first, looking at these graphics can help you distinguish the dynamics of each walk. Then you can apply your understanding to observing people. When we look at people, it is easy to become caught up in superficial detail such as faces and clothing, but I would like to ask you to focus on the walk.

At the beginning of your observations, you may find it easier just to look at the distance between people's feet as they walk. If you can see this clearly, the rest of the process is easy.

Imagine a person walking along a line on the floor. Watch carefully to see where his feet fall in relation to an imaginary centerline. The feet of the people that swing their bodies fall about shoulder-width to either side of the centerline (see the man on the left in figure 4). The people that pull with the muscles in the back of their thighs always place their feet on either side of the centerline (see the man in the center in figure 4.) The ones who fall forward hit that centerline with their heels (see the man on the right in figure 4). These details may seem insignificant, but if you can focus on these simple differences, I can open up the minds of each of these people for you to understand easily. I promise!

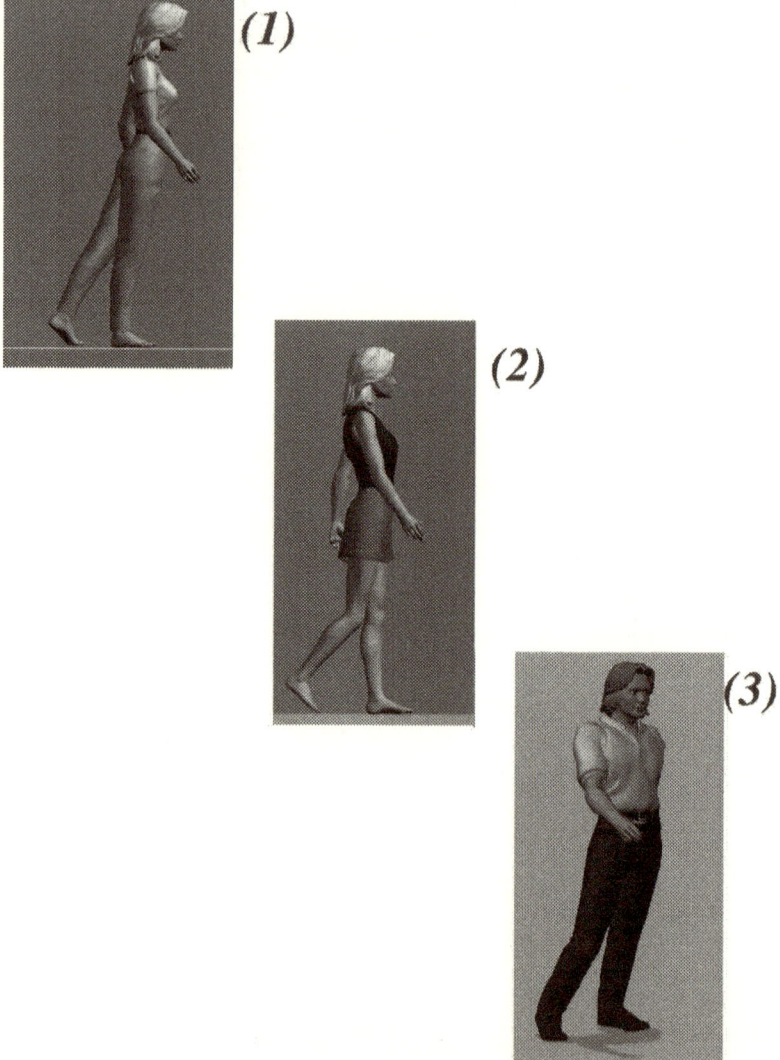

Figure 5: (1) Some of us walk with all of our attention focused on where we are going. (2) Some of us walk with all of our focus on where we are coming from. (3) And some of us walk with all of our focus on what is around us and how we are in relation to our world.

First, where do all these differences come from? Do they always mean the same things? In my original observations, I had no clear answer, but training as a mime had taught me many valuable lessons. One of them is that our bodies are the tangible record of how we have done things physically for a lifetime. What I call "muscle recruitment patterns" refer literally to which muscles our bodies naturally call upon to do any physical movement. It is all "written" in the relative strengths and weaknesses of our muscles.

As I studied people, I would also look at how they held themselves erect, how they walked, how they used their feet and the general shape of their musculature. I began to make the connections and see the ways in which these characteristics reflected what they did in their lives. All I had to do was trace things backwards.

For example, if I wanted to mime a person who has been waiting for 48 hours in a train station, it was not sufficient just to slump down and look tired. Too obvious; good art should always seek to go deeper. I would instead begin by sitting very erect, imagining my train ready to come in. As the imaginary time stretched on, I would relax one set of muscles after another and care less and less about looking normal. After an imaginary several hours had passed, my body would end up in a posture that told tales of muscular fatigue countless battles between each muscle group and the force of gravity relentlessly pulling me down.

In much the same way, you can do a "character regression" from any adult you may see back to the child he might have been. As you observe someone who is walking with widely separated feet and shifting from side to side, can you imagine how he might have looked as a small child walking in the same way? Now go back a bit further in your imagination to see him even younger, as an infant crawling on his hands and feet in a half-crawl, half-walk—almost as if he wants to stand upright but is afraid of being knocked over.

Return to America

After five years of intensive study in Paris, I returned to America and toured the East Coast with a smattering of dance troupes. In time, I was asked to teach university-level master classes in mime at Harvard, Princeton and New York University. As it always had been, my life was a blur of activity. The one constant throughout the chaos was the work I did as a physical trainer for other dancers. Ever since my days at Marquette University, I had been known for having a really good sense of balance, and fellow performers often turned to me for help in fine-tuning the muscles involved in their own body balance.

By 1985, I had opened a private gym in a Soho loft in New York. I began providing intensive one-on-one training to an array of Wall Street tycoons, ordinary people, rock stars and actors. By this time, I fully understood that certain body types utilize, as well as avoid using, certain muscles to accomplish physical tasks. More importantly, I was able to predict in advance how any given client would perform a specific exercise. Some performed well doing all of the back and shoulder exercises, yet would have difficulty with the abdominal and chest exercises. Various people seemed to hold themselves upright by predominantly using the back muscles, while others used more of the front body muscles to do so. Still others used the muscles along the sides of their torsos.

I began to study the muscle recruitment patterns that were showing up in the different bodies I trained. It all eventually completely made sense. Three types of body movements logically called for three types of body musculature. I saw—and could prove—the existence of at least three. Furthermore, every single one of my clients fell perfectly into one of three specific groups!

This in itself was fascinating, but what really rocked my world was finding out the similarities shared within each of the three Bio-Types. Members within each group were amazingly similar; not just in their bodies, but also in how they thought, learned, took in information and reacted to personal situations! I immediately shifted my intense (some may call it "obsessive") focus to studying these similarities and how mental/emotional problem-solving mechanisms were reflected in the physical methods of problem-solving. For example, I found that if an individual "hurled" himself through a sit-up, I inevitably found that he "hurled" himself through an emotional problem.

Almost thirty years of working with people had taught me to focus less on the externals, such as clothes, etc. and more on the posture held by their bodies. I eventually began to extrapolate backwards, trying to get a clear picture of who they must have been as a young child to better understand who they were when I met them as adults. As a specialist of body movement, I would always end up asking myself the same question about each of these people: How did he first get to his feet to stand erect for the first time?

This question turned out to be essential. The body you inhabit today works the way it does as a direct result of how you first learned to use it in response to your environment. The way you first went about these early movements reflected the way you saw yourself and your relationship to your world. This is why the act of climbing to one's feet is so critically important. The muscles you discovered and first developed created a domino-like effect that caused some muscles to develop and others go largely unused.

This pattern of discovery and development led to the evolution of which muscles were to become most available to your body, causing certain muscles to be stronger than others. As a result, the primary postural support muscles that we initially depended upon to stand have shaped how we move for the remainder of our lives.

Becoming upright is the single defining act that separates bipeds from quadrupeds. In an evolutionary sense, the higher we can get our head, the easier and faster it is to view danger and therefore the more time we have to defend against attack. The more time we have, the less we need to rely on teeth and claws. Thus, the greater the distance between our head and the ground, the duller our claws and teeth and therefore the more we are forced to rely on our brain's ability to process visual data, solve problems and inform our body how to behave. The way we move tells everything about who we are.

Taking It on the Road

Before I knew it, I was field-testing my observations on the general public. Every time I identified someone's Bio-Type, I would predict what sort of person he would be and how best to interact with he. I would immediately experiment with my predictions to test their validity by starting a conversation. This is something I had been doing all throughout my difficult developmental years, but never before had I tried to codify my methodologies for use in human interactions.

You see, I had discovered that the process of walking is either a process of falling forward a little and catching oneself on the forward foot; a process of pulling oneself forward using the muscles in the back of one's thighs; or it is a side-to-side torso-swaying process. Hence, with the emergence of the three body types: the "Forward Faller," the "Backward Faller," and the "Torso-Sway Walker," Bio-Typing was officially born.

2

Remembering the Child—Understanding the Person

"Fixed muscular patterns in the body are central to [each] person's way of being in the world. They (the muscles) form in response to family and early environment."

—Ron Kurtz, M.D. and Hector Presera, *The Body Reveals*

"I am not smooth, for my life has not always been smooth. I am not perfectly balanced, for my feelings are not always balanced. I am not symmetrical, for my actions are not symmetrical. My muscular strength is not equally proportioned throughout my body, as my interests are not equally distributed throughout my life."

—Ken Dychtwald, PH.D., *Bodymind*

Life revolves around movement. Your brain may do all the thinking, but your body turns thought into action. Writing involves the use of finger muscles, and speaking requires that you somehow expand your lungs and breathe. Even sleeping requires that you bring your body to a resting position.

These examples go on forever. Humans constantly recruit muscles to move their bodies; this is an obvious fact of life. How various people used their bodies to do the same tasks, however, is what fascinated me from a very early age on. When I began to analyze people's movements carefully, I noticed that the differences among people were not only dramatic in the realm of movement, but also in the realm of personality, and these differences were Bio-Type-specific.

14

To explain, people that primarily carry their weight on the balls of their feet seem to constantly fall forward in whatever they do. Others carry their weight on their heels and are much more observant. They look, and then they move. People of a third type have an even weight distribution between the balls of their feet and the heels, but these people stand over widely separated feet. They approach everything in life from that strong base and are hard to shake, so to speak.

Could there be a definite, demonstrable link between physical movements and personality? There is a link between handwriting and personality, so mustn't there also be one between the way people use their bodies and their personality? Most medical and exercise textbooks say there is only one way to breathe and to bend the torso. Do you agree?

I do not. We will see in this chapter that there is not one, but three sets of functional mechanics of body movements—as in entirely different ways to do the same things. You will begin to see how they dramatically differ from one to another. I will show you the link between personality and body movements. I will also give you an understanding of the key personality traits for each of the Bio-Types and how you can apply that understanding in your relationships, in the business world and in raising your children.

No Instruction Manuals Here

There was once a famous ad for a prominent financial publication. It read, "Money: Unfortunately, it does not come with instructions." We could easily say the same thing about the body into which we were each born. It did not come with an instruction manual. We had to figure out how to use it all on our own.

It all started when we opened our eyes for the first time. We found ourselves in a new body, and it was entirely up to us to figure out how to use it. First, we discovered fingers and feet. Next, we began to realize that these were connected to us. Then we began the quest for control over our body. The world around us filled with exciting sounds and sensations that called out to us. Fairly soon, we discovered that the higher we lifted our head, the more we could see, smell and hear. In time, our crib became too small to hold our curiosity. Raising our head as high off the floor as possible became more and more of a full-time preoccupation. It slowly led us to the next step: How could we get our feet under our body and bring ourselves upright over them?

If we all had gotten up onto our feet in the same way, we would all use the muscles in our body the same way. Yet we clearly do not. Why is this?

Muscle Choices: What Bio-Typing Is All About

The human body is an engineering phenomenon. It is built for survival. Each of our organs, limbs and muscles is designed to be of maximum use. Each of our muscles has a primary task it is best designed to perform. There is a "best possible" muscle or set of muscles, and there is usually a secondary set that can be used instead if an injury to the first set occurs. "Redundancy" is the term I use to describe this phenomenon. For example, the toes and ankles are naturally designed to provide balance for our torso and to compensate for the unevenness of the earth we walk on. If for some reason, however, the toes and ankles become disabled, slight bending of the knees can take this function over and do a decent job. This is what redundancy is all about. Just as the brain is not limited to one specific method of organization, you are never limited to any one unique set of muscles to perform any given movement.

We have all learned our own ways of doing things. Sometimes we use our body as it is intended to work, deploying primary systems to perform a task they are naturally supposed to do. At other times, we use secondary systems—consciously or unconsciously—because we find them more available. For example, if you have always walked using a push-off from the ball of the trailing foot, you will have developed an easy, natural strength in the calves. Thus, the muscles of your feet will be easily available for balance. However, if you have always used your hamstrings to pull yourself forward and used little of your calf muscles, the most available balancing muscles in your body will be in your slightly bent knees.

Every time we came upon the need to do an action, our bodies should have discovered the best possible muscles for that action. This is not what actually happens. In our earliest discoveries of our muscles, possibly with breathing—perhaps even earlier in utero—each of us discovered certain muscles first and then began to use them. It is as if the pathways between the brain and the first muscles discovered for a particular movement became 'hard-wired' as it were, thus more available for subsequent movements, and more available to assist other muscles for other movements further down the chain. We began to use them for almost everything we did. Because of our initial choices of postural support muscles and our reliance on them, certain other muscles became relatively less easily accessible. The person who discovered back postural support muscles to breathe uses his back muscles to lift the head up higher, to walk etc. The heavy reliance upon his back muscles makes his frontal muscles less available.

So why did some of us use more of the frontal muscles and others more of the back muscles?

Your Body Speaks Your Mind

There is an old martial arts saying, "The body follows the spirit, and the spirit follows the body." It means that the way we feel about ourselves reflects the way we see ourselves, and the way we see ourselves reflects the way we feel about ourselves. It also means that the experience we have of being inside our body flows directly from the way our muscles are holding us. As you will soon see, the way we do things with our bodies reflects precisely the way we do things with our minds. If we hold our weight forward over the balls of our feet, ready to leap into action, so do we also hold our mental focus ready to commit to tackling new problems quickly. If we hold our weight back over our heels, we are probably more likely to take the time to assess a problem and the possible solutions first, before we jump in.

These differences in the process of learning to stand and then to walk are not merely accidents of nature. They are inspired by your essential temperament as a child. They are a reflection of the relationship you had to your world then, and it did not stop there. The child you were grew up to be the man or woman you are today.

What is the relationship between how we use our bodies and how we use our minds? I realized something very simple during my research: We first learn problem-assessment and actual problem-solving on a physical level. Only later do we learn to apply what we learned with our body to mental and emotional problem-solving, thus the body-mind connection. Our first adventure in problem-solving was as an infant, trying to get our little body out of the crib and into our mother's arms. Today, getting up and walking across a room is an automatic process, but back then, it was our first great challenge. We were taking on the conquest of gravity and the secrets of locomotion.

What Does This Have to Do With Interpersonal Relationships?

Just as John Bowlby suggests in *Attachment and Loss: Loss, Sadness and Depression* that the nature of early internalized experiences with caregivers forms the prototype for later relationships; I propose that internalized childhood experience forms the prototype for later relationships within each Bio-Type. If you can learn to see the little child that became the full-grown person in the adult standing in front of you, relate not to the costume he is wearing or the role in life he is playing but to the child he really still is underneath, then you are using the information encoded in his body.

Remember that in many ways, our personality is based upon how we approach everyone and everything in our world. A person's hopes and fears are displayed in the way in which he holds his body. At all times, the attitude that he has about each new experience is written in the tensions held in his body. Check it out! If you watch yourself or anyone else doing just about anything physically, you will see a perfect reflection of exactly how you or another person solves problems mentally. For example, the person who hurls himself through a physical exercise, such as a sit-up, is likely to hurl himself through other tasks as well. You might say that accomplishing a task by charging energetically toward its completion worked well once, then why not use the same dynamic approach the next time? If this sounds simplistic, maybe so is life, as well as our learned approach to it.

Remember those theorems we were taught in school to solve math problems? Things like $A^2 + B^2 = C^2$? In a similar way, our bodies developed their own bio-mechanical "theorems," and our minds applied these same formulas to our ways of thinking and accomplishing things elsewhere in our lives.

So where did we develop these "theorems"? Each one of us got up onto our feet in one of the three possible ways. You have probably never examined this process in yourself, a process that has become automatic. Let's look at it now. Do you place both of your feet together on the floor and use them and your back to push you away from the floor, or do you naturally use your hands and your feet to climb?

There are not one, but three possible muscles recruitment patterns to bring you to a standing position. The reason for this is purely physiological. Three groups of postural support muscles dictate our body alignment. These are the muscles along the front of the body, the muscles along the back of our body and the muscles along the sides of the body. This pattern repeats throughout our musculature. The deltoids, or shoulder muscles, have three parts: the anterior (front), the medial (center) and the posterior (back). Any book on human physiology will show you pictures of these muscles. The same goes for the gluteus (buttock) muscle and the thigh muscle.

Ideally, the postural support muscles should all exert equal force in holding up our spines. The fact is, however, that it never actually happens this way. Some of us use more of the frontal muscles; some of us use more of the back muscles. Just look at any group of people standing. Some are holding their spines slightly arched backwards, and others are hunched slightly forward. The differences may appear slight at first, but if they were glaringly obvious, I would not need to point them out.

Why do different individuals use more of the back postural muscles or more of the front ones? Within the scope of my work, I have found the reason for this is actually linked to each child's essential temperament, which was developed because of his first choice of muscles he engaged when he first established his movement patterns.

Let me show you why. Picture a toddler starting to climb up independently to a standing position. There are Forward Fallers, Backward Fallers and then there are Torso-Sway Walkers.

Forward Fallers

Figure 6: Forward Fallers primarily use the front muscles of their body to climb up onto their feet.

People I call "Forward Fallers" in my Bio-Typing system are naturally adventurous children. Early on use walls, armchairs or whatever is available to view their world from a higher perspective. Using a convenient piece of furniture to get to their feet, they move forward from table, to chair, to sofa without much attention to how—only where—they are going (see figure 6). As children, they must have felt completely secure and protected in their environment. They were not overly concerned about independent vertical stability; they are more interested in getting somewhere. You can see this in the way they hold their weight over the balls of their feet and lean slightly forward, even when they are standing still. They hold their weight well forward over the balls of their feet, ready to leap into action.

When they walk, there is a definite forward-falling quality to their gait. Forward Fallers develop predominantly stronger muscles in the front of their bodies. Their legs are used primarily to catch the Forward Fallers and prevent them from falling forward, not to pull themselves forward. They rely predominantly upon their front postural support muscles for vertical support. As adults, Forward Fallers still walk in a forward-falling manner and live their lives in a similar fashion.

Forward Fallers lead with their hearts and throw themselves into and through their life's challenges and experiences. They are always moving toward the next objective and bounding ahead. Their mental focus is much the same, about getting somewhere. The biomechanical "theorem" they discovered in early childhood may have been something like this: "What's next + forward motion + effort in a chosen direction = new experiences." Forward Fallers commit to tackling new problems quickly and are eager for new experiences and sensations. Forward Fallers want a goal. They work the rest out as they go along.

Forward Fallers tend to be impulsive, are often led by their emotions and usually find themselves frustrated when dealing with people who move in a more methodical way. Forward Fallers like to focus on their dreams so that others can see the future as they do. This "What's next + forward motion + effort in a chosen direction = new experiences" way of being can be seen in almost everything they do. When they are interested in possibly buying a book, they open it to the first page and start reading, just to see if they like it. They do the same thing when they meet someone new. They just start talking to see if they enjoy being with that person. Life will never be dull for them, because even before they have settled into one thing, they are already leaning toward their next experience. Forward Fallers are doers and adventurers.

My friend Michael is a Forward Faller. He always seems to be perched on the balls of his feet, ready to jump into something. His mother told me that when he was a child, he was the terror of the neighborhood. He would charge through the homes of his neighbors, and anything not placed higher than he could reach was fair game for his exploration and possible destruction. He was always inventing new adventures in which to engage the other children. This entailed investigating places like the abandoned building behind the fire station or building new structures out of boxes and boards. He was not afraid of much. He was always getting cuts and scrapes doing things that none of the other kids would dare to try.

Figure 7: My friend Michael is a Forward Faller. He always seems to be perched on the balls of his feet, ready to jump into something.

Backward Fallers

Figure 8: Backward Fallers primarily use the back muscles of their body
to climb up onto their feet.

Those I call "Backward Fallers" are self-reliant and independent as toddlers, and they approach life much more cautiously. They learned to get up onto their feet without using any external support. Backward Fallers first discovered their two feet, got them planted on the floor and then climbed up onto them.

These children relied on their back muscles to straighten their spinal muscles and lift their heads as high as possible to see more of their world (see figure 8). By standing up in this fashion, they supported all their weight over the heels of their feet. From then on, their tendency throughout life would be to hold themselves upright using predominantly the back muscles. Once these children gained confidence in maintaining their balance and staying erect, their next step was to observe the world around them. Many parents recount stories of these children learning to walk when they were not looking—as if they used that time to practice before showing it off. One day the child was experimenting, the next he was a skilled walker. Something may have caught their attention, but their approach remained cautious. First, these children looked carefully, then methodically planned their route and approached the object of their interest, one-step at a time.

To walk for the first time, Backward Fallers placed one foot in front of them, and then pulled themselves forward using the hamstrings (upper back of the thighs). These children did not much use the balls of the feet for balance. As adults, they still walk in a methodical, systematic manner and live their lives in a similar fashion.

Backward Fallers solve each problem, face each challenge and attain each goal in a methodical fashion, using the biomechanical "theorem": "Thorough observation + detailed planning + action = achievement of a goal." They look before they leap. Backward Fallers are observant and careful, ever appreciative of details other people often miss. They have an instinctive tendency to take in all the information they can regarding any given challenge or experience, then go forward in an orderly, step-by-step manner.

Backward Fallers prefer to read the cover, table of contents and the back of a book before they commit to buying it. Likewise, they examine a new acquaintance in the same way before they commit to a way of dealing with him. Relationships require forethought, and Backward Fallers observe a new person from as many angles as possible before giving out their phone number. More than likely, a Backward Faller works in a field that illuminates others through his words or images, such as journalism or teaching. A Backward Faller may even be an artist or visionary who naturally sees more detail than others do.

Chris, my wife, is a Backward Faller. She has a very straight back and stands with her weight on her heels and her head slightly tipped back. She is always observing people and things. Chris can pick up a newspaper or a magazine and read the whole darn thing. She is interested in just about everything and everybody. Chris is a photographer, producer and therapist, who seems to see observe more closely than other people. She is also very independent and likes to discover things on her own. Even if I try to direct towards a more efficient movement skill, she will usually try it out her own way first. Then—maybe—she will ask me to show her how I do it. Chris also thinks as she walks, one-step at a time.

Figure 9: Chris, my wife, is a Backward Faller. Observe how she has a very straight back and stands with her weight on her heels and her head slightly tipped back.

Backward Fallers have predominantly stronger muscles in the back of the body. Before being willing to take action, they will probably take a moment or two to consider and assess a problem. They are observant and careful, and they tend to go forward in their lives in an orderly, systematic manner. Backward Fallers become keen observers of life and share their observations with others.

In dealing with Backward Fallers, you should allow them to take in information about you so that they are able to see who you are, what you have to say and where you are coming from. Do not push a Backward Faller into getting him to talk about himself when, in fact, they are the ones wanting to hear about you.

Torso-Sway Walkers

Figure 10: Torso-Sway Walkers use their hands and feet to climb to a wide-based standing position.

Those of the third Bio-Type, called "Torso-Sway Walkers," are completely different from the other two. They crawl fast and furiously to get where they are going, using all four of the extremities to pitch forward until that is just not enough and they need to get up onto their feet. (See figure 10). Torso-Sway Walkers may also have feared falling or being knocked down, and for this reason, they crawled for a longer time than the other Bio-Types. Torso-Sway Walkers often may be children who grow up with many siblings, busy households, or perhaps even in a situation or neighborhood where there was stiff competition or physical danger. For whatever reason, these children feel the need to establish a firm stance that physically translates into a strong, wide base of support. The biomechanical "theorem" they discovered in early childhood may have been something like "Goal, measured against danger or challenge + astute effort = stability and goal achieved."

Once they begin to walk, Torso-Sway Walkers seem to swing their legs forward using the muscles along the sides of the body, giving a side-to-side ambling quality to their movement. They develop a very stable standing position with feet wide apart and develop an equally strong position in their world.

Torso-Sway Walkers confront each new situation using the biomechanical "theorem" "Goal, measured against danger or challenge + astute effort = stability and goal achieved." They naturally come from a strong power base and shift fully into each turn on their journey forward in life. When they take a stand, they really mean it, and they do not back down easily.

To buy a book, Torso-Sway Walkers first check out who the author is and what other books he has written. They want to examine where the author is coming from and then decide whether it is compatible with his own criteria. In the area of relationships, Torso-Sway Walkers will allow others into their world if they do not pose too much of a challenge, are not oppositional to this Bio-Type's perspective and appear safe and stable.

In their work, Torso-Sway Walkers will probably be good at more than one thing, perhaps even changing careers several times in their lives. They often exemplify the term "Renaissance man."

My friend Veronica is a Torso-Sway Walker. She was the youngest child and the only girl in a family of boys. As a child, she was petite and felt the presence of "big" people all around her. Her brothers often fought with each other and sometimes with her. Amid their feistiness, she feared being knocked down. Veronica crawled on all fours until she managed to do a kind of hands-and-feet crawl, or bear walk, that led directly into a rising to full standing position over widely spread feet. Veronica was not about to let herself get knocked down! She was outspoken and extremely determined as a child—especially for her size—and she remains so today. Veronica always stands as if rooted to the ground; her feet planted firmly shoulder-width beneath her, chin jutting out. When we have discussions, Veronica does not back down easily. I remember her telling me that in her childhood, she was once ordered to remain at the dinner table until she finished her vegetables. Needless to say, she didn't. After three hours, her mother had to give up on trying to get Veronica to obey.

Figure 11: My friend Veronica is a Torso-Sway Walker. She always stands as if rooted to the ground; her feet planted firmly shoulder-wide beneath her

Torso-Sway Walkers have predominantly stronger muscles along the sides of their body. They stand with their feet spread widely, and because of this wide stance, they walk with a shifting side-to-side effect. Their strong physical positions are reflected in their mental attitudes. Torso-Sway Walkers do not back down from a position easily and confront each new situation from a strong power base.

The key to effective communication with Torso-Sway Walkers is finding a point of commonality between the two of you upon which to build a foundation. Remember that Torso-Sway Walkers are going to look at you from their place in the world and then decide if you fit into it or not, simply by the way you present yourself. So let them present themselves first to you. Sit back, be patient and allow Torso-Sway Walkers to weave you into their world.

Walking in One of These Three Ways.

Humans learn to walk in one of three ways. The method we each chose to solve the primary challenge of learning to walk started a chain reaction inside our bodies that established relative muscle strengths and weaknesses. If your back muscles are stronger than your front-body muscles, your back muscles will hold your back in a tighter grip, arching it a little. If the front-body muscles are the stronger, they will hold your spine slightly bent forward.

Why is this important? Imagine holding a heavy weight in your hand with your elbow slightly bent. (See figure 12.) If you start with your arm slightly bent, it is easy enough to bend your arm to curl the weight. Now imagine the arm fully straightened with the weight in your hand. If the arm is too straight to begin with, the bicep is too stretched-out to easily engage. When you try to bend your arm, you will find your shoulder muscles begin to engage.

In just the same way, if you arch your back, your abdominal muscles are too stretched-out to engage, you will use the next most available muscles to bend your torso. In this case, torso flexion will naturally occur by use of the upper quadriceps. If the back is too tight, the abdominals will be too stretched-out to engage easily. In a person's postural alignment, if the front, back and side muscles are not balanced, the stronger muscles will be easier to engage than the weaker. This is why two people who engage in the same action can be using different muscles from one another.

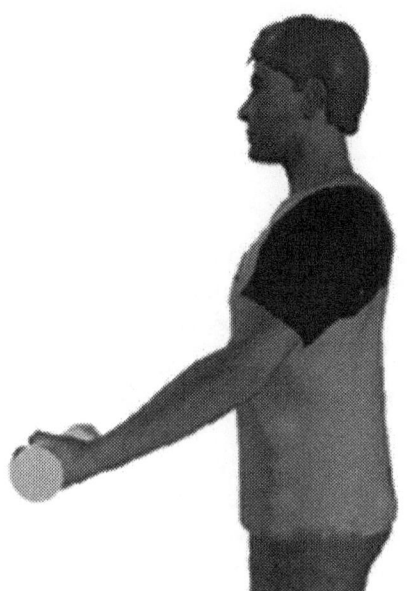 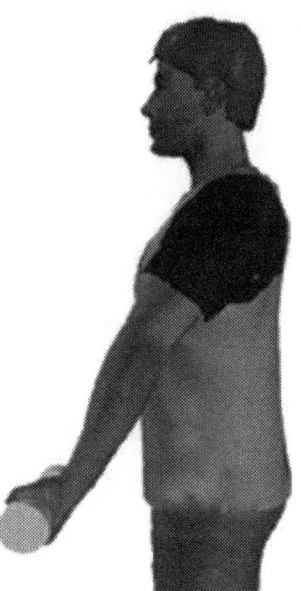

Figure 12: Imagine holding a heavy weight in your hand, with your slightly bent. It is easy enough to bend the arm against the weight if you start with the arm slightly bent. Now imagine holding the weight with the arm fully straightened and trying to bend it.

The muscles we used the earliest in life to motor us forward developed more than those less relied upon. Because a stronger muscle is denser and therefore shorter, these stronger muscles gradually pulled the bones of our spines into the postural alignment we have today. Consequently, for each Bio-Type, the primary postural alignment muscles made other muscles either more or less available. An individual with strong back muscles will naturally stand with a slightly arched back. A person with more developed muscles in the front of the body will naturally stand arched slightly forward. Our bodies are the tangible record of how we have done things physically over our lifetime, written in the relative strengths and weaknesses of our muscles. Imagine a body builder who does push-ups every day. He might tend to be so overdeveloped in the pectorals that his shoulders are always pulled forward. Yet another person who does too many lat pulls in a workout might develop a great V-shaped torso and a permanently arched back.

The Scope of Bio-Typing

Our Bio-Type reveals our personality by showing us how we do things physically. Bio-Typing provides a window into the minds of others, teaching us to examine how their bodies do—and have always done—physical things. Remember the "theorems" presented earlier?

Each of us is constantly offering and being offered a wealth of intimate information about ourselves and about each other. This information goes far beyond what we merely want others to see when they look at us. Once we begin to understand the differences in the functional mechanics of our individual bodies, we can begin to understand and acknowledge the reasons these differences exist, and what they might suggest about our minds.

Bio-Typing can therefore be used to enrich personal relationships in many ways and to achieve more effective communication. Knowing how people are likely to solve physical problems gives dramatic insight into how they will relate with us. Their methods of interaction come from early self-discovery and the mindset created by choices that their bodies made to stand up onto their feet and thus approach the world.

Once you understand how another person views the world, the guesswork is removed, and you can plan an appropriate strategy for interacting with him. For example, if you know that your spouse or sweetheart is a Backward Faller, it is probably not a good idea to charge in and begin enthusing about your grand idea to redecorate the house. The Backward Faller's biomechanical "theorem" established in early childhood is: "Thorough observation + detailed planning + action = achievement of a goal." Their interactive technique is: "Meet someone + observe to see how he presents himself + observe where he is really coming from = let him in a little or give him a chance to reveal more, before closing the door or accepting him."

The most effective approach would be to present the idea slowly. Show how you have thought out each detail of the project and give the person time to process each step. Simply hitting him or her over the head with your plan will do nothing but push the person away. How Bio-Typing applies in the field of love and personal relationships develops further in Chapter 8.

In the business world, your ability to read in advance how a person takes in information and what his concerns are ultimately dictates your ability to present the appropriate facts to him. For instance, imagine that you have just entered a business meeting to sell a concept or product. If the people you are speaking to are Forward Fallers, they will be especially interested in what the future will look like in terms of your product or concept. If they keep stopping you and ask for detail and clarification point-by-point, chances are you are dealing with Backward Fallers.

Knowing this, you would be wise to proceed in your discussion by using the clues your audience has presented to you. You would indulge these Backward Fallers, explaining things in a systematic step-by-step fashion.

If you figured out the people you are dealing with are Torso-Sway Walkers, chances are they are not going to hear you until they are sure you have heard them first. Remember a Torso-Sway Walker's biomechanical "theorem": "Goal, measured against danger + a little careful effort = stability and a goal achieved." His interactive strategy will be: "Listen to someone + determine where he is coming from + determine if he poses a threat + determine how what he says coincides with where the Torso-Sway Walker is coming from = let the someone or the someone's idea in, or push him or it away.

The best course of action would be to create an opportunity that allows this Bio-Type to let you know where he sees himself coming from before you present your concept or product. Wait for him to speak his mind fully before you continue. Then find a part of what he has to say about his vision or philosophy of life that relates to your presentation, and weave it into your pitch. How Bio-Typing applies in the business world is fully covered in Chapter 9.

What can Bio-Typing teach us about our children? The beauty of raising your children with an understanding of how they see themselves in relation to their world is that by recognizing the way they use their bodies and what approach they naturally take toward life, you can help them to discover the world in a way that is perfectly suited to them. You can also help them to develop physically and emotionally in ways that would otherwise go un-nurtured.

For example, if you understand that your child is a Forward Faller, you can teach him to stop to observe the things taking place around him before diving in. If your child is a Backward Faller, you might want to help him to develop the confidence to jump forward to try new things by learning to trust his body more, rather than let his mind dissect every step of the way and thus allow doubt, fear or uncertainty paralyze his actions. If your child is a Torso-Sway Walker, in under-standing that his naturally wide-standing position reflects a fear of being knocked down, you could encourage him to play, jump and take chances. You can encour-age him by reminding him often that he is unique, important and protected. How Bio-Typing applies between parent and child is fully developed in Chapter 10.

To gain this knowledge, all you need is to really see yourself in the mirror of body movements and then learn to look at others in the same way. So let us begin. Chapter 3 introduces five easy self-diagnostic tests to help you determine your Bio-Type. It is fun and can reveal much about yourself and others.

Forget horoscopes. Bio-Typing will prepare you for social, business and family interactions like nothing you have ever encountered before.

3

Discover Your Personal Bio-Type

If you want to understand a neurotypical person, ask a person with autism, because we have had to figure out why normal people do what they do in order to interact with them. When you look at a person to try to understand him or her, you must learn to develop a context for organizing the data you have before you.

Now comes the fun part. Discovering your own Bio-Type is easy. You can do so in one of two ways: Use the quick "one-test" analysis or the full method of five tests. The first one takes seconds. The rest take less than fifteen minutes. Each approach requires only that you perform simple, everyday actions.

Why are there two methods? The most telling difference between Bio-Types, the distance between the heels, is so clear that the walking test alone will most often tell you which group you belong to. This is the easiest one-step test. It may not be sufficient in all cases, but most often, it will be.

Method number two involves five tests. The advantage to it is that you get a lot more evidence of how your Bio-Type pervades every action your body does. This method includes the quick "one-test" analysis discussed above and leads you through another four. Test number two looks at what your body does when you bow. Test number three shows you that we do not all breathe in the same way. Test number four challenges your balance on one foot. Finally, test number five asks you to sit on the floor and get back onto your feet as naturally as you can. Understanding the outcome of each test increases your knowledge of what to look for when you want to identify someone else's Bio-Type.

Whatever method you decide to use, the rules are few. Please make sure you follow them.

Important Considerations

Note that you may have practiced disciplines, such as sports or dance, that can create minor variations in the alignment of you feet, but these are minor distractions. Do not become distracted! Although the primary muscle recruitment patterns you developed in childhood never change, what you have done in life can create "overlay" movement patterns that can alter a certain aspect of the tests. Studying classical dance, for example, is likely to cause a little more turn-out in the feet when walking and standing.

Ask a Friend to Observe You

You can test yourself on your own by using a large mirror or a video camera. I would strongly recommend, however that you instead ask a friend to observe you. We rarely see ourselves as clearly as others see us. We are part of our own shell, a piece of our own puzzle, and so it is difficult for us to have perspective. A friend will be better able to make an objective judgment.

I regularly have experiences with people that highlight the importance of this point. Typically, I ask someone standing in front of me to describe the position of his without looking down at them. "Of course they are turned out," is often the answer. This is usually followed by some justification such as, "I am a dancer you know." Well, this person is often in for a surprise. When we both look down, we notice that his feet are not turned out at all but are quite parallel!

Relax, and Be Your Natural Self

When new clients first walk into my studio, I clearly notice how their body moves. Later on, when I ask them to walk naturally toward me, they sometimes do so differently than they did at first. For example, where their feet earlier fell clearly on each side of an imaginary centerline, they are now crisscrossing it. This happens because we often walk and move differently when we know we are being observed.

Men instinctively lift their chest and straighten up. Women tend to put their natural attributes forward and exaggerate the movement of their hips and jutting chest. Whether you decide to test yourself alone or with the help of a friend, put aside all of your preconceptions, relax, and be your natural self. Remember this is a test, not a fashion show, so there is no need to walk to impress. It is important to walk as you walk every day and breathe as you have always breathed. Do this as many times as need be, until you are confident that what you are doing is the real you.

Do It Barefoot, or Wear Shoes Without Heels

Regardless of your Bio-Type, wearing high-heeled shoes pushes your weight over the balls of your feet and forces you to move in a forward-falling manner. Just watch fashion models on the runway and you will see the exaggerations in the lateral movements of the hips and the centerline placement of the feet under their centerlines caused by the high heels.

Try All the Options Given

Whether you go for the quick "one-test" analysis or the full five-test method, there are three ways of performing each test. Members of each Bio-Type predominantly use one over the other two. How can you tell with certainty which of the three possible ways you naturally do? Try all three. The right one for you will always feel better than the other two. Make a note of the one that feels best.

The more you do these tests and understand the reasons why your body works the way it does, the easier it will be to discover someone else's Bio-Type quickly. The more you understand yourself, the better equipped you are to understand others. Are you ready?

The Quick "One Test" Analysis—Walking

There is no correct way to walk. The act of walking involves so many muscles that even kinesiologists (experts who study the principles of mechanics and anatomy in relation to human movement) find it difficult to say with certainty which muscles are used and in what sequence. Part of this confusion has to do with the fact that different people walk in different ways. Let us see what your body does.

Find an open space, and do this test with a friend, a big mirror or any reflective surface.

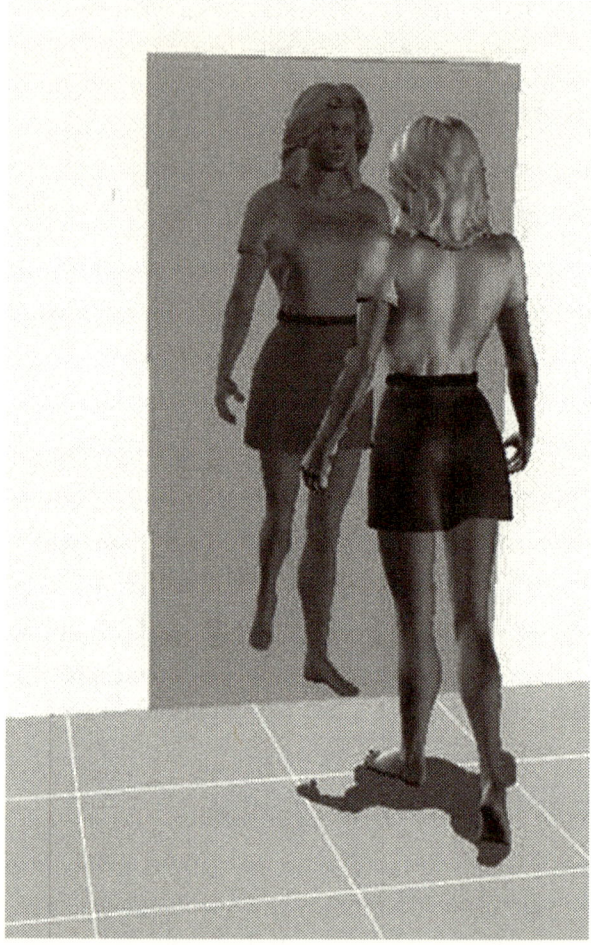

Figure 13: You might want to try watching yourself walking toward a mirror.

Find a line, or imagine one on the floor beneath your feet. You can usually find a line in the pattern of flooring that will work for this test.

Walk along this "centerline" toward, then away from your friend or the mirror and observe where your feet fall relative to it. As you walk, pay attention in order to make the following three observations.

Watch the Distance between Your Heels

As you walk, watch the distance between your heels. How far apart are they?

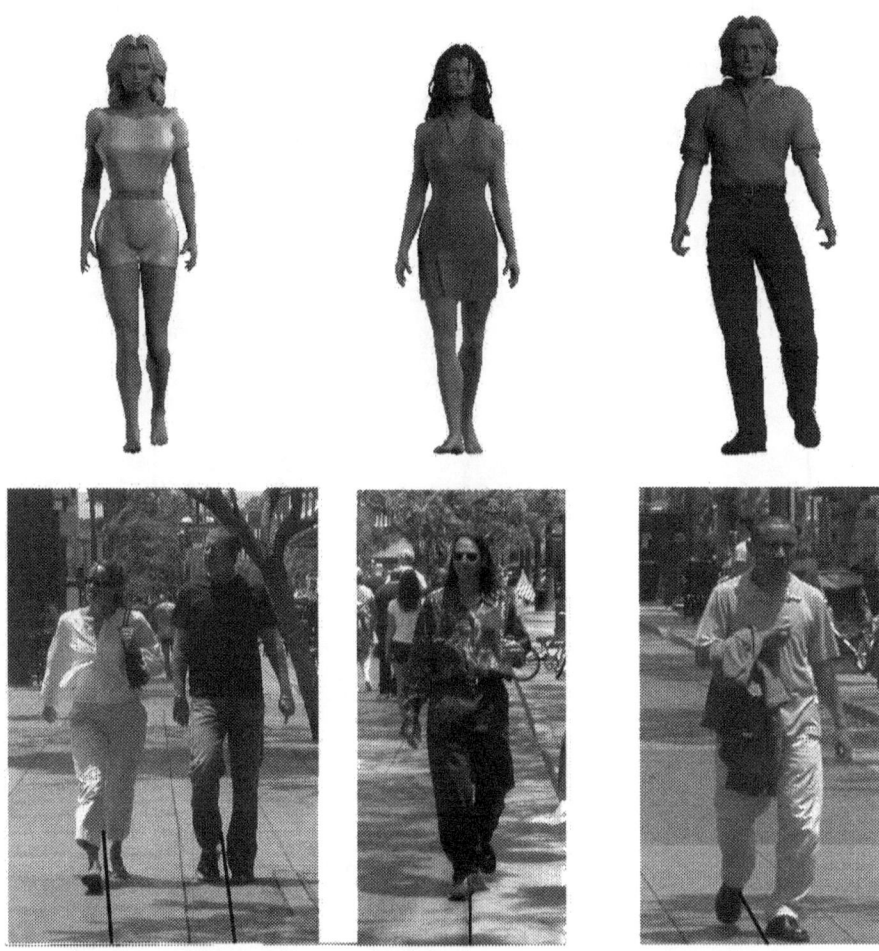

Figure 14: Watch the distance between the heels. Backward Fallers (left), Forward Fallers (center), Torso-Sway Walkers (right).

Some people walk with their heels about two inches apart, feet falling either parallel or slightly turned outward and remaining on either side of the centerline (see figure 14, left). I call these people Backward Fallers.

Others have stronger inner-thigh muscles that pull the legs together. Their feet naturally turn outward and crisscross the centerline, pushing off from the ball of the trailing foot and falling onto the leading foot (see figure 14, center). I call these people Forward Fallers.

In a third group of people, the muscles that pull the legs apart are stronger than the ones that pull them together. As a result, these people walk with their feet about shoulder-width apart and falling dramatically on either side of the center-line (see figure 14, right). I call these people Torso-Sway Walkers.

Watch What You Do with Your Legs

As you walk, watch what you do with your legs (see figure 15.) do you push with the calf of the trailing leg, or do you pull with the back of the leading leg?

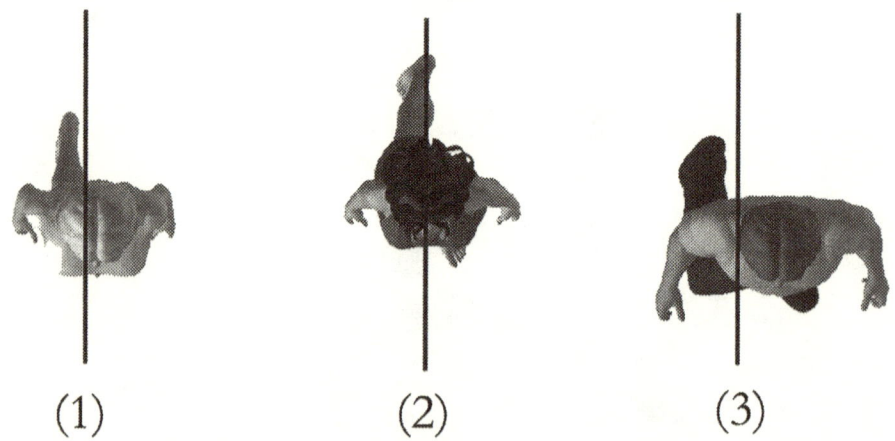

Figure 15: Watch what you do with your legs.

Backward Fallers (figure 15, #1) pull themselves forward using the back muscles of the leading thigh (hamstrings). These individuals can look at the wear pattern on their shoes. It will show mostly at the heels.

Forward Fallers (figure 15, #2) push off with the ball of the trailing foot. These individuals will see that their shoes wear at the ball of the foot as well as at the heels.

Torso-Sway Walkers (figure 15, #3) shift their weight dramatically from side to side as they walk.

Pay Attention to the Movements of Your Head

Does your head move a little from side-to-side, or a lot, or not at all? If you are looking at yourself in a mirror, it can be a little difficult to determine how your head is moving, so just ask a friend to close one eye and watch from a distance in front of you as you approach him.

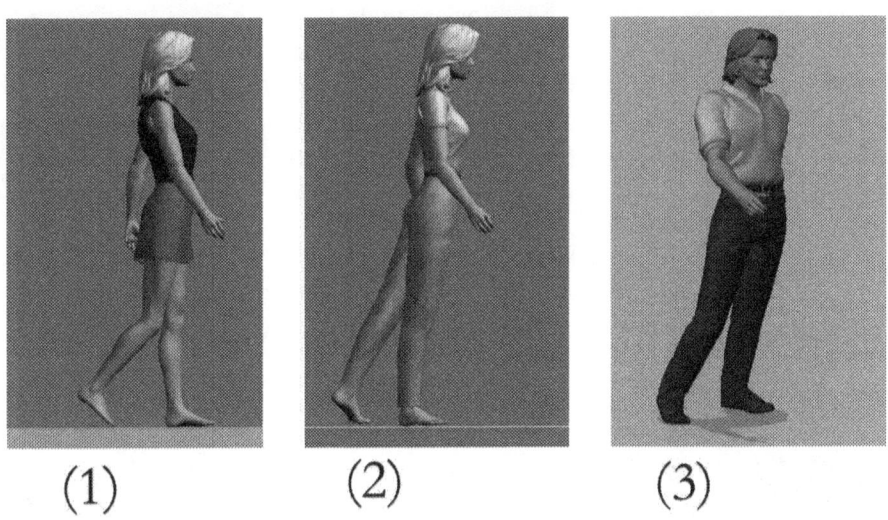

(1)   (2)   (3)

Figure 16: Pay attention to the movements of the head. Backward Fallers (left), Forward Fallers (center), Torso-Sway Walkers (right).

Does your head slightly move from side-to-side as you walk? If so, you are likely to be a Backward Faller (see figure 16, #1.)

Perhaps your head remains centered as you walk. If so, you are likely to be a Forward Faller (see figure 16, #2.)

If your head very noticeably moves together with your whole upper body from side to side as you walk, you are likely to be a Torso-Sway Walker (see figure 16, #3.)

What Is Your First Overall Impression?

Switch off your mind now and let your body talk as you do the test. Forget what you believe and look at the process with new eyes as your body does it. What is your first overall impression?

To get a clear comparison, try this process of elimination. Find a place on the floor or the sidewalk that has a line on it. Walk first with heels landing on the centerline, and then walk with your feet landing about two inches on either side of that line. Finally, walk with your feet falling about shoulder-width on either side of the line, shifting your whole weight from side-to-side. Which method feels easiest and most natural for you? You will most probably be surprised at how different the processes of walking feels when done the way the other two Bio-Types do it. It will probably be a bit of a revelation to discover that there are such differences in the way that different people walk!

Here is a summary of how each Bio-Type normally behaves in the walk test.

Forward Fallers

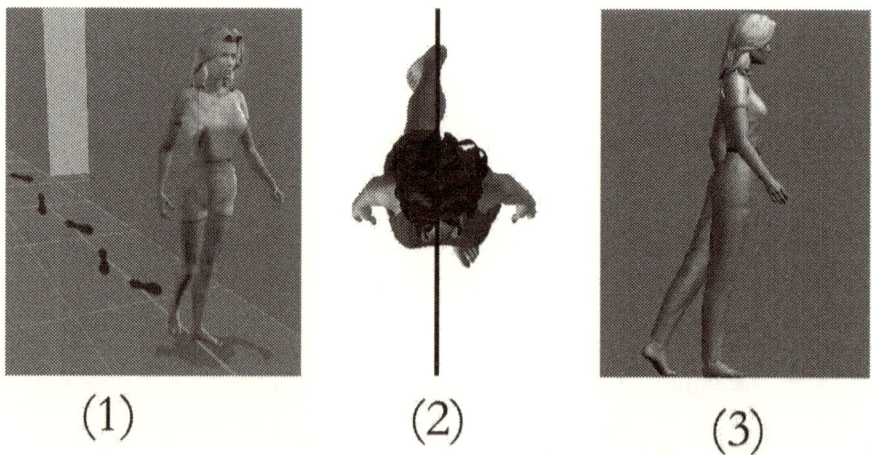

(1)   (2)   (3)

Figure 17: Forward Faller-#1: The heels are very close and almost touching, crisscrossing an imaginary centerline. #2: The head remains immobile, right over the centerline. #3: People from this group push themselves forward, carrying their weight primarily on the ball of their feet.

When I watch my friend Pam walking, I see no side-to-side movement of her torso at all. Even her head remains totally centered, not shifting side-to-side at all. Her feet also tend to be turned outward but her heels fall along a centerline under her. She pushes off with the ball of her trailing foot, falling onto the leading foot Check out Robert Downey Jr. Look at his turned out feet and the way his heels land on the centerline.

Backward Fallers

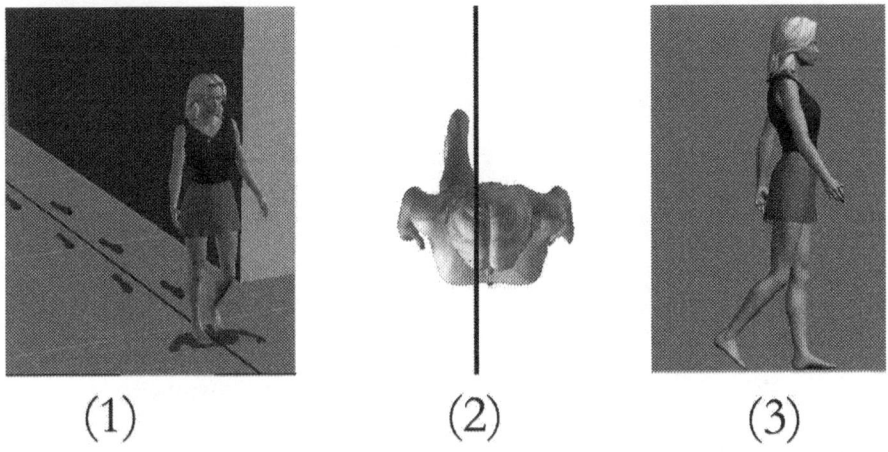

(1)   (2)   (3)

Figure 18: Backward Faller-#1: The heels are about two to 4 inches apart and the feet remain on each side of the centerline. #2: The head is slightly moving from side to side. #3: People from this group pull themselves forward in a straight line. They carry their weight primarily on their heels.

When I watch my wife walking, I see her head move about two inches from side-to-side, her feet falling parallel on either side of an imaginary centerline. She pulls herself forward with the back muscles of the leading thigh (hamstrings). George W. Bush walks the same way.

Torso-Sway Walker

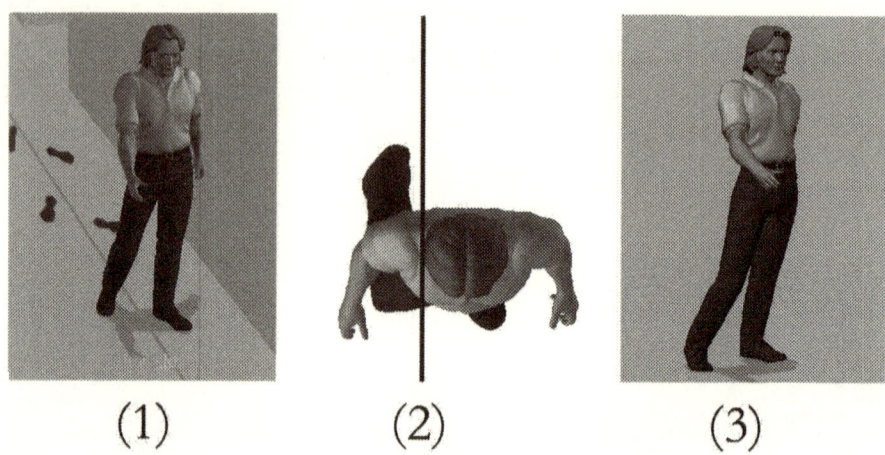

(1)   (2)   (3)

Figure 19: Torso-Sway Walker-#1: The heels are shoulder-width apart,
feet falling on either side of the centerline #2: The head shifts noticeably
(sometimes dramatically) from side-to-side #3: People from this group
pull themselves forward, transferring their whole weight from one foot
to the next, shifting dramatically from side-to-side as they move.

When my friend Will walks toward me, I am always very conscious of the way his body shifts dramatically from side-to-side as he walks. He makes me think of Hoss on the old Bonanza TV series. You can see what I am referring to for yourself any evening on TV if you look closely at either Jay Leno or David Letterman. They, too, are Torso-Sway Walkers. Both have the same side-to-side movements of their heads and bodies as they walk, together with the turned-out feet. Both of them are secure in knowing who they are. This is why they are good at getting other people to talk about themselves.

The walking test alone tells most people what their Bio-Type is. I encourage you, however, if time allows doing the remaining four. I always take my new clients through the five tests myself. Doing so makes for absolute certainty. In addition, the better you understand what the tests look for, the better you will know what to look for when you want to Bio-Type other people.

Are you ready to carry on?

Test Number Two—Bowing or Torso Flexion

The forward bending of the torso is such a common action that we rarely realize that different people do it in very different ways.

When I bow after a performance, I often do so in theatrical manner, with a foot behind me and a flourish of the front hand. I saw Rudolf Nureyev bow like this once, and it stuck. There are actually a surprising number of different ways to bend our bodies forward in a more natural bow.

Just ask any personal trainer what variations he or she gets when asking a client to do a full sit-up. Many people seek to hook their feet under something. This is a sign of weak and underdeveloped abdominals. They do this because the muscles that are strongest and most available in their bodies for bending forward are not the abdominals, as many may think, but the upper thighs. If they cannot find something to hook under, their straightened legs become the counterweight that the torso uses to bend forward.

The accessibility of the muscles along the front of the body can vary greatly from one individual to another. Some people have such strong lower back muscles that these strong muscles have really tightened their back and made the muscles along the front of their body difficult for them to access. If the lower back is hyper-extended by overdeveloped lower back muscles, then the abdominal muscles are less available, and these people use the upper thigh muscle instead.

This may all sound like theory to you. Let's get practical and see what your body does.

Position yourself turned three-quarters toward the mirror or your friend, jump into the air, and do not move your feet after you land. This is to find your natural stance. Pay very close attention to the distance between your heels.

Now, bow slowly forward, until your head is at the same level as your hips or slightly higher. Some of us bend at the waist, and others bend at the hips. Where does your upper body bend?

If You Naturally Bend at the Waist

Figure 20: Forward Fallers naturally bend at the waist (left). Their abdominal muscles are naturally stronger than the other two Bio-Types, and they usually do not need to hook their feet under something (i.e., engage their quadriceps) to get up in a sit-up exercise (right).

If you naturally bend at the waist, you are probably a Forward Faller. This is what members of this Bio-Type always do (see figure 20, left). To see the same torso flexion tendency of your body during sit-ups, lie on your back, bend your knees, keep your feet on the floor, and try to bring your upper body to a full sitting-up position several times (see figure 20, right). The abdominal muscles of Forward Fallers are naturally stronger than those of the other two Bio-Types, and they usually do not need to hook their feet under something (i.e., engage their quadriceps) to get up in a sit-up exercise.

If You Naturally Bend at the Hips

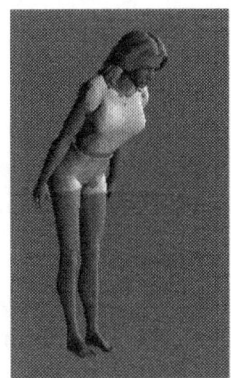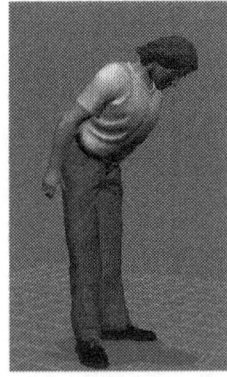

Figure 21: Backward Fallers (left & right) and Torso-Sway Walkers (center & right) naturally bend at the hips.

If your feet come up off the floor a little and/or your body is bending naturally at the hips, you are probably either a Backward Faller (figure 21, left) or a Torso-Sway Walker (figure 21, center). You can tell the difference by looking at your feet. Remember when I previously asked you to jump and not move your feet after you land? The purpose of this was to find your natural stance. The determining factor between these two Bio-Types will be the distance between the heels. Backward Fallers tend to have the legs together, two to four inches apart (figure 21, left) and Torso-Sway Walkers have them shoulder-width apart, about 10 to 12 inches (figure 21, center).

If you are a Backward Faller or a Torso-Sway Walker, you may find that you are able to do many sit-ups, and therefore believe your abdominals must be very strong. They may well be, but I would invite you to try the following variation to confirm it for sure. As you go through a sit-up, bend your knees, do not hook your feet under anything, separate them to about three feet apart, and stop halfway up at about 45 degrees. If you suddenly lose all the "abdominal strength" you had, then I have made my point. It was actually your upper quadriceps (thighs) that were flexing your torso, and this is what you were led to believe was your "abdominal strength."

Test Number Three—Breathing

Breathing is something that everybody does every day, all day long, so who really notices what naturally happens when we breathe—unless it is not happening? Most people do not know what muscles are involved in the action of their own breath. Even fewer notice the differences in the ways others breathe.

One of my clients in Los Angeles is a pulmonary specialist. Medical school never taught him anything about breathing. Here is what he says about Bio-Typing in relation to this subject:

"I am a practicing medical doctor who is a lung specialist in Los Angeles and have been involved in taking care of patients with a variety of respiratory or breathing problems. With the knowledge I have gained on the proper use of the diaphragm and other breathing muscles for myself, I became interested in how these principles could be applied to my patients. Johnny and I are investigating the role of Johnny's unique method of respiratory muscle-training in patients suffering from emphysema."
—Ralph Potkin, M.D.

Have you ever watched someone important to you take a deep breath and sigh? Many people arch their backs when they inhale. Other people spread their chest to the sides. Yet others expand their diaphragm downward.

I remember my friend Bill facing a man who had just threatened him with harm. Bill stood there, his chest spreading to the sides and contracting as he tried to contain his anger. He looked like a bull about to charge. Bill is a Torso-Sway Walker. My wife and I were there when that incident happened, and I can clearly remember her chest going up and down as she breathed. She was clearly arching her back with each inhalation. My wife is a Backward Faller. As for me, my belly seemed to expand as I inhaled. I am a Forward Faller. Each one of us breathes so differently!

In the best of all possible worlds, each one of us would naturally use all the best available muscles to breathe as deeply as possible with each breath. To do so, we should always first lift the sternum (chest), then expand the ribcage to the sides, and then fill the lower part of the lungs by expanding the diaphragm downward. These three actions call upon three different sets of muscles. Each of us, however, uses more of one and less of the other two. Which muscles does your body naturally use more?

What You Are Looking For

Remove whatever clothes you need to take off in order to make sure you can see your chest and abdomen very clearly. Inhale deeply and observe.

Do you breathe primarily into your abdomen? Forward Fallers (see figure 22, #1) expand their abdomen to force the dominant breathing muscle, the diaphragm, to come down and create a vacuum that will suck air into the lungs. This is what I call "belly breathing."

Do you breathe primarily by lifting your chest up? Backward Fallers (see figure 22, #2) most often lift their chest using spinal muscles. They use almost none of the downward expansion of the diaphragm and very little of the intercostal muscles (between the ribs) to spread their ribcage laterally (side-to-side).

Do you breathe primarily by spreading the chest laterally? Torso-Sway Walkers (see figure 22, #3) primarily spread their ribcage laterally, using muscles called the levatores costarums. However, they forget about the downward action of the diaphragm as well as the lifting action of the spine.

Try all three options. Which one feels easiest for you?

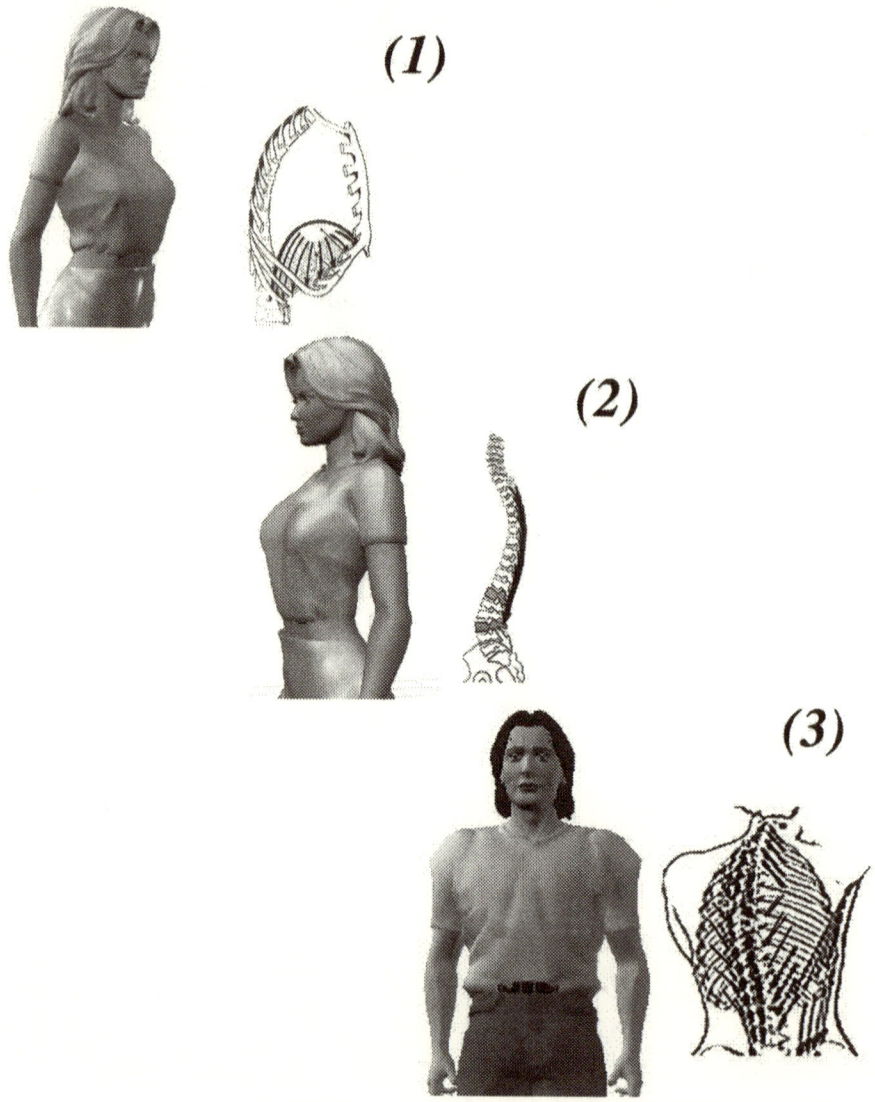

Figure 22: Forward Fallers (1) first expand their abdomen when they breathe. Backward Fallers (2) most often lift their chest, using spinal muscles. Torso-Sway Walkers (3) primarily spread their ribcage laterally, using the levatores costarums.

Frequently, the lack of strength in the muscles that tuck pelvis forward has an extreme influence on the diaphragm's ability to expand downward between breaths.

Here is an interesting experiment you might want to try in order to see how well your diaphragm expands downward between breaths.

Sit on a chair in the normal way for your body. Now exhale a series of the syllable "huh," as many times as you can in a row. This is called the "breath of fire" in various yoga systems. You may find that you are quickly running out of breath and have to inhale soon. Now do it again, but before you inhale, tuck your pubic bone forward and lift your chest. Does the shift in the alignment of your pelvis make the lungs seem to refill with air automatically between "huhs"? This is because the tucked-under pelvis allows the diaphragm to expand downward on its own.

Test Number Four—Balancing on One Foot

Some people have great natural balance, and some do not. When the latter group tries to stand on one foot, they begin to wave their arms about and move their torsos from side-to-side. The others, however, just rise easily and stay there, stable and unwavering. Part of the reason why is that we each use different muscles to help us to maintain our balance.

The act of maintaining balance either on the whole of one foot or (even trickier) on just the toes of one foot requires that we make quite a few movements to adjust. It is like driving a car; we are constantly making little corrections on the steering wheel to continue driving in a straight line. We need to compensate for the unevenness of the road. Similarly, we need to compensate for the imperfections of the ground when we are walking. Different sets of muscles can be used for this task. Some of us use little lateral movements of the ankle; others use movements of the knees.

In my many years as a professional dancer, I studied balance. I discovered that different people use different muscles to maintain balance, whether they are doing a dance position or walking in high heels. Our ability to balance comes from how we walk.

Because some people pull themselves forward when they walk, using the back of their thighs, they tend to keep their legs just slightly bent. If the leg you are balancing on is slightly bent, you will find that the process of maintaining balance takes place primarily at the knee level instead of the ankle.

Other people push off with the ball of the trailing foot with each step and therefore develop strong calf muscles. Because these muscles control the ankle, these people use their ankles to balance and are able to keep their knee locked.

What You Are Looking For

Pull your pants up above one knee, and make sure that it remains completely visible. Stand on that leg and rise onto your toes. Either you can put the leg that is in the air in front or behind the one on which you are balancing. Now try to balance there.

Do the test now. Pay very close attention to the knee and the ankle of the standing foot. What does your body do? What primary and secondary balance muscles do you reach for?

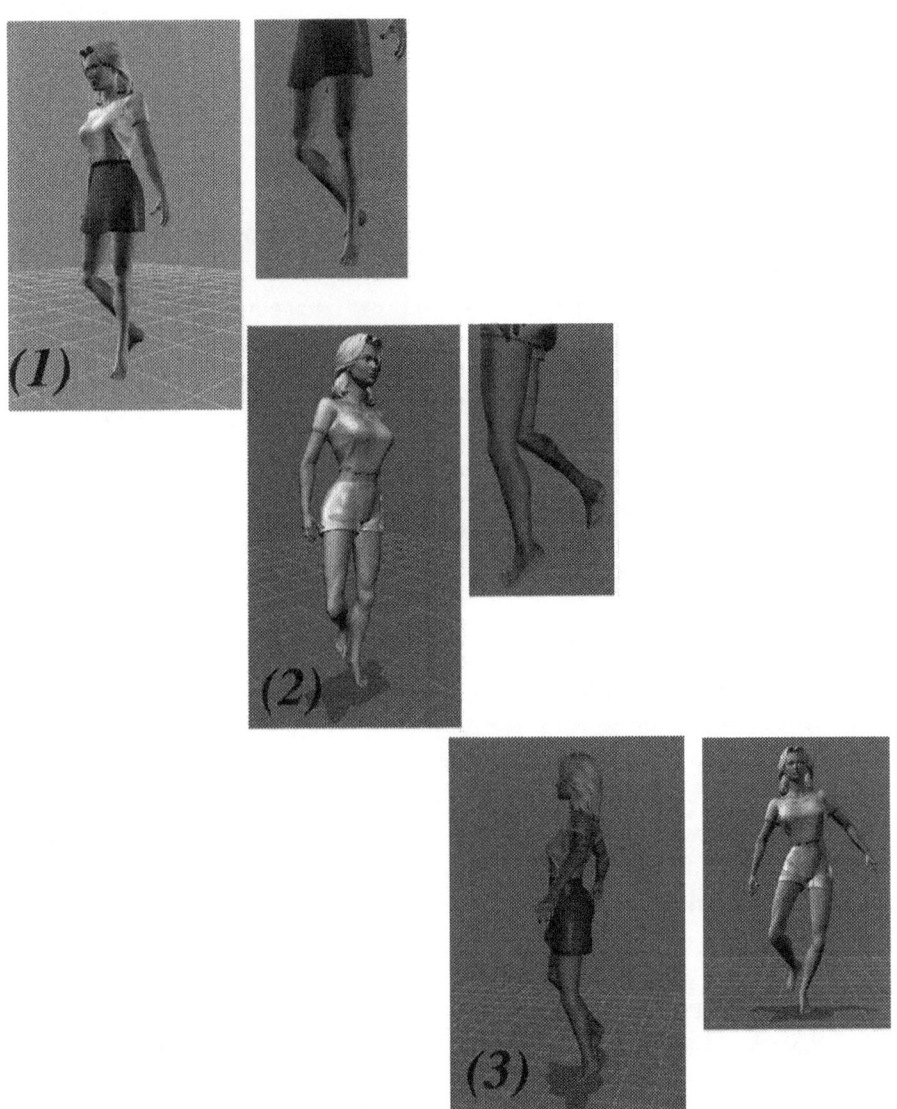

Figure 23: Do you (1) naturally keep your knee locked and use little movements of the ankle to maintain balance? Or do you (2) maintain a slightly bent knee and use little movements of that knee? Or do you (3) use larger side-to-side movements of the torso?

When standing on one foot, if you tend to keep your knee locked and use movements of the ankle to maintain balance, you are probably a Forward Faller (see figure 23, #1.)

Backward Fallers (figure 23, #2) and Torso-Sway Walkers (figure 23, #3), on the contrary, keep the supporting knee slightly bent and use it to balance instead of the ankle. If your knee is doing all the work, you are one of these two Bio-Types. To find out which, look next at your torso while you try to stay balanced on one foot.

As you continue balancing on one foot, at some point you are likely to start losing your balance. The natural human reaction is to move up one level and engage the muscles of the torso in a last attempt to bring back equilibrium.

Pay close attention to how your torso tries to save the day

Do you arch backward? If so, you will naturally tend to fall back when you lose your balance, and thus, you are a Backward Faller (see figure 23, #2.)

Do you move your torso from side-to-side? If so, you are probably a Torso-Sway Walker (see figure 23, #3.)

Test Number Five: Sit Down on the Floor and Get Up

Something important happened when you first climbed up onto your feet to see more of your world. You were on the ground crawling, and you naturally wanted to get your head up as high up as possible to see as much as possible of this world you were born into. You had a choice of muscles you could use, and not all of us used the same ones. The choices your body made were both a reflection of how you saw yourself and the first step in a chain reaction that determined which of your muscles would be most accessible to you—and subsequently, the most used—for the rest of your life. Some of us used more of the muscles along the back of our spines to lift us up. Some of us swung the legs around to the sides in a hands-and-feet crawl on the way to standing. The rest of us used external support, a chair or a wall to boost ourselves, climb up and launch ourselves into our world.

Let us see if we can go back into the history of your life written in your muscle recruitment patterns by looking at what your body does in this test today.

What You Are Looking for

Please sit down on the floor. I would like to you to try to get up in what you feel is the most natural way for you.

Ideally, we want to try to let our bodies remember our childhood. Getting to our feet from a seated position on the floor is a very important action. In contrast to how we first got up, we may have later learned a way that is more elegant than the one we first discovered and used as a child. As a dancer, I want even this action to be graceful, so I cross my legs, then turn in a full circle as I rise to my feet. I learned to do it this way in a dance class, and I always do this, as long as I am not too tired. When I am, my "elegance monitor" switches off, and my body takes over. Then get up to a standing position just as I used to as a child. Try turning off your elegance switch.

You want to "get back to your roots." This is not always easy. Sit down on the floor and remember: No elegance. Simply try get back onto your feet in the most natural way.

Figure 24 shows each of the three ways through which children first learn to get to their feet. Do the test now, and try each of them a few times. Which of the three feels most natural?

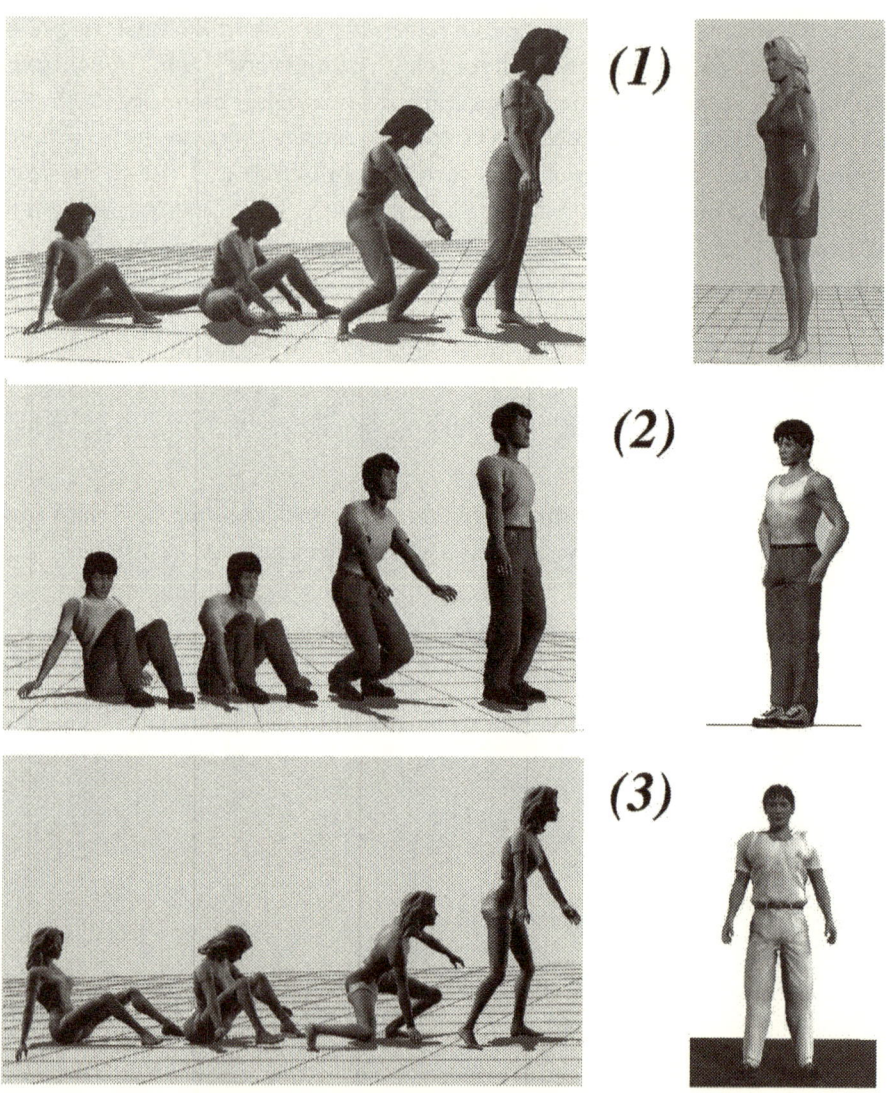

Figure 24: (1) Forward Faller, (2) Backward Faller, (3) Torso-Sway
Walker.

Does it feel most natural to keep your hands off the floor, roll across a bent knee
and step onto the leading foot up to the standing position? Are you a person who
naturally stands heels together, feet turned outward? If so, then you are probably
a Forward Faller.

Are you more comfortable bringing both feet under you and pushing up to get your body off the floor, eventually balancing your buttocks directly over your heels? Do you then push on both legs and use your back to straighten up? Once up, are your feet about two to four inches apart, with your weight on the heels? If so, then you are probably a Backward Faller.

Does it feel most natural to do a sort of half-crawl, using at least one hand on the floor to push and climb up to a wide-based standing position? Do you naturally stand in this solid and secure standing position? If so, then you are probably a Torso-Sway Walker.

What Is My Bio-Type?

Which of the Bio-Type specific choices did your body make most often in the course of these tests?

Which category did you most often fall into the majority of times? Was it Forward Faller, Backward Faller or Torso Sway Walker?

Congratulations! You have just established your personal Bio-Type.

Do not be surprised or puzzled if there are some inconsistencies in the choices that your body made. Most people have one or two overlaid patterns of movement. We often learn new ways of doing things throughout life, and this will overlay our natural movement patterns. You should find, though, that in at least three out of the five tests, your body's choices fall into the same group. If this is not the case, I suggest that you try again and have a friend watch you this time.

Read on! Chapter 4 describes the full profile of Forward Fallers, Chapter 5 describes the Backward Fallers, and Chapter 6 describes the Torso-Sway Walkers.

Should this information be of further interest to you, you can find a detailed physiological explanation of how and why your body behaved the way it did for each of the five tests at <http://www.biotyping.com>

4

Forward Faller Bio-Types

Figure 25: A Forward Faller, me.

When we are young, our bodies are strong and they work well. As we get older, we begin to lose our eyesight. Then our hearing starts to fail, and our muscles begin to get weak. To me, our bodies are like library books that we take out on loan. Like books, they have a lot to teach us if we study them. When I have to give my body back, I do not want to have left any chapters unread.

I refer to your Bio-Type as a Forward Faller because when you first got to your feet as a child, you did so with a serious goal in mind: to get a closer look at whatever it was that caught your attention. What it took to get there was irrelevant. These were the children who fell face first, and consequently often had scabs or dings on their hands and faces. They often tripped as children, not seeing the uneven ground, and learned to recover magnificently.

The act of getting to your feet in the first place was just a problem to solve on your way to something more important than the act itself, something that attracted you. Consequently, you fell naturally into a forward-falling walk, pushing off with the ball of the trailing foot and catching your weight each time you fell forward onto the leading leg. This is the reason why you, the Forward Faller, carry your weight over the balls of your feet.

You probably saw something that totally captured your attention, and on the way, you used a handy wall or chair to help climb to your feet. You got one foot under you and used a cross-lateral movement of the torso and opposite arm to roll onto the other foot. If you were to sit down on the floor right now and stand up again, you might find that you still get up in the same way you did as a child.

As a child, you naturally crawled in a cross-lateral fashion. By this, I mean the left arm and right leg alternating with the right arm and left leg. Because of your cross-lateral way of crawling as a baby, alternating the use of the left and right sides of your body—and therefore of your brain—you can easily shift from the left (analytical) side of your brain to the right (intuitive) side. You often make important decisions based upon your feelings.

Because of this ability, you probably have chosen a profession where you are always doing new and exciting things. You are by nature a doer, a fixer, a builder, and probably a leader, whether or not you wait for others to catch up before you charge into the next new thing. You might well be an inventor, designer or entrepreneur.

Once over your feet, you did not stop to establish independent vertical support before you fell forward into the next step. When you first climbed onto your feet, you were on your way toward something that attracted you. For you, climbing to your feet and the process of walking were just a means to an end, the end being whatever caught your attention. Today, you are still forever falling forward into the next relationship, the next new experience.

In a way, Forward Fallers are not about what they are but about where there are going. When you first got up, you were not thinking about getting up, you were thinking about getting somewhere or getting to something. In a psychological way, you are always moving to the next action or experience. You are always going forward and are ready to move, ready to plunge into a new thought, action or decision. Just look at your weight poised over the balls of your feet, ready to move. Where the other two Bio-Types keep their weight over the back of their feet, you do not. They will need to shift forward before stepping out; but not you.

Because of a lifetime of using calf movements to push your body forward, you tend to have good balance and characteristic fluidity in mental or physical situations.

You are often led by your emotions, but you can make decisions based upon concise logic as well. You are naturally impulsive and you are forever reaching for your dreams. You, the Forward Faller, dive in with the end goal as the full focus and deal with obstacles on the way as they come up. You do not always take the time to consider the consequences of your action.

If you look at your feet, you will find that you naturally tend to keep them slightly turned-out. Thus, you are open to many things simultaneously and may find it easy to do two or three different things at the same time. You are probably also comfortable dealing with several people at the same time. You have left/right dominance, a cross-lateral ability of taking in facts from one situation and applying them to another.

Your torso bends naturally at the waist, and when you rotate your torso, you keep your balance and do not lift one hip, as the other two Bio-Types tend to do. You can roll with things without losing your balance.

Your weight is naturally forward over the balls of your feet. You are always ready to move forward, and if threatened, you are likely to make a move.

You are not sequentially oriented, and so might find yourself doing more than one thing at a time and applying the lessons learned from one thing to the process of doing another. You possess great fluidity and balance in mental and/or physical situations. You can become frustrated with people who have to go step-by-step when you can leap ahead and fill in the blanks afterwards.

When you wake up, you are pulled forward out of bed by the prospect of what you are going to have for breakfast or what is waiting for you at the office.

Famous Forward Fallers

Brian Ferry
Annie Lennox
Robert Downey Jr.
Marlin Brando
Mahatma Gandhi

See the turned-out feet and the forward attitude of the bodies in figure 26? Charlie Chaplin wanted to be in movies. He was first a stage performer. Then he made the movies. He wrote them. He directed them. Then he ran the studio that made his movies. He also wrote the music for the scenes he created. Then he organized the movie industry into a business owned and run by the actors, called United Artists.

Gandhi wanted to change his country. He forged ahead in any way that he thought might work to initiate the changes he envisioned. He did not hesitate to put his own body on the line to achieve what he envisioned.

Figure 26: Famous Forward Fallers: Charlie Chaplin, Mahatma Gandhi;
Athena, goddess of the hunt.

You can see examples of the Forward Faller clearly in ancient Greek statues from Sparta. The Spartans saw themselves as warriors ever-ready to leap into battle. This is certainly not to say that there were not plenty of Backward Fallers and Torso-Sway Walkers in Sparta, but the Spartan image that has survived through the statues seems to glorify the Forward Fallers, depicting the daring and bold-ness of the warriors.

The Forward Faller Personality

Goal-Oriented

Goals motivate the Forward Faller, not the steps to get there. When they wake up in the morning, they think of what they are going to have for breakfast or where they have to go that day. By the time they get up, they are already mentally on their way out of the bedroom or out of the house. Throughout the day, their nat-ural tendency is to clearly envision and reach for their dreams, always diving in with the end goal in mind. They deal with obstacles on the way as they come along. Once they solved the problem of forward locomotion as a child, they charged into the next challenge, confident that if they pushed forward, their body would come up with another on-the-spot solution. Today, they are the type of person who leaps into the new and the unknown, leaving behind everything to pursue it, with the primary concern: "What is happening now?" "What is our next big thing going to be?" It can sometimes be hard for others to catch up with them before they charge into the next new thing.

Forward Fallers can become frustrated with people like Backward Fallers, who have to go step-by-step. This is because the natural tendency of Forward Fallers is to leap ahead and fill in the blanks *en route* or afterwards.

Visionary

Forward Fallers have great dreams and visions of what could be. They excel at visualizing possibilities, and they follow a horizontal thinking process (what you can do once you "get there" or "have it"). They are unfettered by too many reality-based details, and they naturally have the energy to surmount all the difficult details as they arise. Their enthusiasm can be great motivation for people who are uncertain about exactly what they want. Forward Fallers normally choose a profession where they are always doing new and exciting things or changing the world around them. They are by nature a doer, a fixer, a builder, and probably a leader. A Forward Faller is somebody who throws himself across the line to get whatever interests him.

Both Emotional and Analytical

As a child, they crawled in a cross-lateral fashion. This can be seen still in the way they reach out with the left hand while advancing the right leg. This cross-lateral way of moving is constantly accessing the left and right hemispheres of the brain, because the left hemisphere of the brain controls the right side of the body and vice versa. This means that Forward Fallers are likely to be both emotional and analytical at the same time. They tend to act impulsively on feelings to make decisions. Although they are often led by their emotions, they can surprise the people in their lives by sudden bursts of concise logic. Conversely, they can guide their logical decisions with emotional input.

Ability to See the Viewpoints of Others

Their open-mindedness gives them the ability to see the world from the viewpoints of others. In new encounters, they immediately try—and succeed—at creating involvement with others, because they are already envisioning the relationship they want to create. Where another personality might be considering whether to get involved, the Forward Faller is already creating the involvement.

Ability to Multitask

Their brains are not sequentially oriented, and they are usually comfortable doing more than one thing simultaneously. They have a great open-mindedness. They possess great ability to develop fluidity and balance in physical and mental situations. They have the ability to take facts, ideas or solutions out of one context and apply them in a different context, bring a fresh approach to an often-stagnant situation.

Quick to Charge In

If a Forward Faller is a martial artist, he is fast at charging in. That speed comes from the strength of his calves, which he is constantly using when he walks to push himself forward, and thus, his weight is already over the balls of the feet.

If they can withhold their urge do jump in and launch the first attack, there is much for them to gain. They can learn from the Backward Faller to wait for the other person to make the initial attack, so they can use the other person's force against him and take him out. They can learn from the Torso-Sway Walker how to adopt a wide and stable position and take the full weight of an attack. This will give them the power to shift, throw the entire body of the attacker and win. In the event of a conflict, they are likely to be on the front line.

They are likely to be innovators, designers, adventurers, architects or guides. Their natural ability to envision a finished product or an exciting experience will make these kinds of pursuits interesting for them.

A Powerful Ally

Forward Fallers are very powerful allies as long as you can keep them focused on the important dream—your mutual goals. You should enlist these people if you need energy to fuel the realization of a given project. Note, however, that at some point, they will start to see your dream as their own.

A Few Management Tips for Dealing with Forward Fallers

Show Them the "Dream" and Give Them Goals

If you have people working for you, how you manage them and present the parts of an overall task requires different approaches for different Bio-Types. Forward Fallers need to be goal-oriented. They need to be shown the "dream" first, not the details. They work the rest out as they go along. If you want them to work well, give them a goal they can visualize, and know when they have achieved it. This may mean breaking the overall project down into stages and making the completion of each stage a separate goal. Also, give them a little help to work out all of the possible pitfalls along the path because they do not always consider all of the ramifications of a plan. They are so good at seeing the end result that they often do not look carefully at the terrain ahead and will slam into obstacles that Backward Fallers, for example, would have foreseen and planned for in advance.

Let Them Talk. You Listen.

Forward Fallers need to talk about their dreams so you can relate to them. They like to be heard and form a picture of you while you listen to them. Then they decide how to involve you in their life. In dealing with Forward Fallers, let them present themselves. Let them talk. You listen.

Know Your Opponent

Watch out! Even if they wear an attitude of casual disinterest, trust what their postural alignment tells you. As martial artists, Forward Fallers are aggressive and fast. The same applies in real life. They are people who attack quickly and easily, so if you are not ready for that, stay out of their way in case of conflict. This urge to attack can give you an advantage, because they give themselves fully into the movement. They will take quick advantage of any openings that you carelessly leave, but will also fall into any deliberately planned openings that you carefully offer them.

Make sure you are ready when they approach, and beware of attacks from the floor up. These could turn to be powerful. Forward Fallers naturally have good femoral rotation and will not have any trouble pivoting to deal with a sidelong attack. In a conversation, they can open to and take in what anyone is saying, and even apply it to the task on hand.

Forward Fallers—Key Personality Characteristics

They are always ready to "fall forward" and move into action.

They focus on the end result, not the steps to get there.

They address challenges as they appear.

Strengths

They are enthusiastic and are visionaries, great motivators for people who don't know exactly what they want.

They are by nature doers, fixers, builders and often leaders.

Weaknesses

They do not always take the time to consider consequences of their actions; they are impulsive.

They have a tendency to start projects but not finish them; they would like to finish before they even start!

Tips for Successful Conversations

Let them speak. You listen.

Talk about the dream and its benefits, not what it will take to attain it.

How to Unsettle a Forward Faller

Take a slow step-by-step, analytical approach to everything.

Reminders for Other Bio-Types

Extra Considerations if You Are a Backward Faller

Moderate your desire to help Forward Fallers work out all of the possible pitfalls along the path. You do not need to point them out before the Forward Fallers get there themselves. There will always be time when they are stuck to show them all the things you are good at stockpiling in anticipation of the needs of the future. Telling them today what is going to be a problem tomorrow will seem to them like a lack of faith, when it is really only loving support.

Extra Considerations if You Are a Torso-Sway Walker

Be aware of your tendency to be a little too concerned about the way things are and not open enough to the way someone else might see how things could be. The "my way or the highway" attitude you might hold to can sometimes get in the way of hearing a new idea or plan that might really appeal to you.

Extra Considerations if You Are a Forward Faller dealing with another Forward Faller

If you both want to rush ahead and solve problems, you can try taking things learned from Backward Fallers and bring a more step by step approach into the conversation. Learn from the Torso-Sway Walkers and carefully reiterate your stand and your objectives. You might be surprised to discover that the Forward Faller you are talking to has just assumed that you were operating on the same intention that he was and find out that there are important differences to examine together.

5

Backward Faller Bio-Types

Never decide in advance what winning is going to look like. You deserve so much more than that.

Figure 27: Two Backward Fallers.

I refer to your Bio-Type as a Backward Faller because when you first got to your feet as a child, you did so in concentrated, step-by-step manner. This process included the discovery of each of your feet. You probably fell backwards many times before eventually reaching your upright position. The parents of these children are thankful that diapers made a great cushion. If they did fall forward, they certainly would have landed on hands and knees, not as a plank like the Forward Fallers did.

When you did get up onto your feet, you did so entirely independently of any external support. If you were to sit down on the floor right now and stand up again, you might find that you still get up in the same way you did as a child.

By now, you may have learned new ways to stand, perhaps not. As a child, you were forever trying to get your head up as high as possible in order to see everything there was to see in the world around you. This may have a lot to do with why you probably chose a profession where you illuminate ideas, plans, information, etc. for others. You are a natural observer, and you like to share your observations with others. Perhaps you are a teacher, journalist, photographer, producer, or perhaps in some other profession where you guide others to see things you naturally take in. You are also a good organizer.

You have always been extremely independent and self-reliant. You do everything in an orderly sequential fashion. You look first, decide where you want to get to, then proceed to go about getting there one-step at a time.

You are either very logical or very emotional, but rarely make important decisions based upon your emotions. You rarely take ill-considered actions, and people who make decisions based upon emotion irritate you. In fact, once you make a decision, you try hard not to let your emotions get in the way of what you have decided. And when someone else tells you how to do something "correctly," you do it your own way first, even if there is a good chance they know more than you, just to try your way first.

You test other people's ideas before you subscribe to them, and you do not like to be pushed or pressured. When you wake up in the morning, it is best for your spouse if he or she does not try to hurry you out the door. You want to wake-up and prepare for the day in an orderly manner.

You excel at prioritizing things in your life and always proceed in an orderly, methodical fashion toward what you want, just the way you walk. You would rather deal with one thing at a time in sequence, rather than all at once.

When people approach you with something they want you to become involved in, you wait to hear them out before you offer your own ideas.

If someone threatens you physically, you step back and wait to see what he is going to do first before reacting. You are the same way in all things. You listen to what the other person has to say or wait to see what he is going to do first, and then you respond. You like to be well prepared for most things you decide to undertake.

By the way, do you notice you are reading this with a natural mental "stepping-back," maybe even a desire to argue?

When you bend your body, whether for bows or for sit-ups, you naturally bend at the hips. When you do full sit-ups, you like to hook your feet under something. When you do push-ups, your elbows are wide to the sides. You do not have naturally good balance.

You probably tend to get lower back pains or have a chronically tense back of the neck, because these are both places for tension in your body.

If you do martial arts, when you rotate your body (as in to avoid an attack), you tend to lift one hip and so become at the risk of falling. This makes you vulnerable to sidelong attacks in a fight or to "off the wall" references in an argument.

A gesture pattern you have is that you tend make a really strong point, then break contact. For instance, when you get angry with someone, you hurl your feelings at him and immediately break contact. You might shout, "Just leave me alone!" and then immediately turn to walk away.

Famous Backward Fallers

George W. Bush
Henry Ford
Margaret Thatcher
Martin Luther King Jr.
Michael Jordan
Mick Jagger

Oprah Winfrey
Ronald Reagan
Sean Penn
Victoria Principal

Martin Luther King Jr. may have had a dream, but he also saw the steps necessary to achieve it. He took each of those steps with forethought and determination. He planted his weight over each of the steps he took. Henry Ford envisioned a whole way of building cars in its entirety, and then set about adding the steps together to achieve his goal. The same applies to Margaret Thatcher. First, establish a vision or a plan then follow each step required needed to get there.

Figure 28: Famous Backward Fallers. Martin Luther King Jr., Henry Ford, Margaret Thatcher, a statue depicting a Greek man from ancient Athens.

You can see examples of the Backward Faller clearly in the statues depicting ancient Greeks from Athens. The Athenians saw themselves as keen observers and analyzers. This is certainly not to say that there were not plenty of Forward Fallers and Torso-Sway Walkers in Athens, but merely that the Athenian image that has survived in the writings and the statues seems to have glorified the Backward Faller's qualities of observation and logic applied to all things.

The Backward Faller Personality

Everything One Step at a Time

The adult you became still walks in a methodical, step-by-step manner and lives his life in a similar fashion. Woe be to those who try to rush you into unpredicted actions or positions! The same goes for those who try to rush you out of bed in the morning and out the door! You want to take the waking-up process in an orderly manner. First, you need to open your eyes, and then look around the room to establish where you are now and where you are going next. Then you may plan your day: what to do and how to do it. Then and only then, do you normally get up and go about your business. The same process applies everywhere. During the day and in all your activities, you look first, decide where you want to go, and then proceed to get there. You observe the goal and then put it aside for a while to focus on the step-by-step process of arriving to it.

You can become frustrated with people like Forward Fallers who seem to rush into things without planning. Your natural tendency is to do everything sequentially and with proper forethought.

Planner and Organizer

You know how to prioritize the things in your life and are an efficient organizer. You excel in packing your suitcase (at least a day early). You are good at anticipating and preventing potential problems. The last thing you want is leap into the unknown. "What?" "Why?" "Where?" "When?" and "How?" are questions you ask yourself or others on a regular basis.

Analytical Thinker

As a child, you crawled in a unilateral fashion, using the left arm and left leg alternating with the right arm and right leg. Today you use either the left (analytical) or the right (intuitive) part of the brain. This means that you can be either analytical or intuitive, but not usually both at the same time. You seldom make important decision based upon your emotions and very rarely take ill-considered actions. In fact, people who make impulsive decisions based upon emotion irritate you. Once you make a decision, you try hard not to let your emotions get in the way of what you have decided, even if you find your decision causes you emotional difficulty.

Single-Focused

If a situation requires it, you can multitask. However, as a rule and given the choice, you would rather deal with one thing at a time and in sequence, rather than all at once. Many Backward Fallers hear this and are quick to question it, but consider what I mean by my assessment. If you are working at a computer and someone says "Excuse me, I need to talk to you," you will not make yourself immediately available in that moment. First, you save your work or close the program, maybe put the computer to sleep. Then you are ready to deal with the new situation. In other words, you shift away from the task at hand to shift toward the new one easily enough, but you do so in an orderly manner, one step at a time. Yet at the same time, a part of your brain will still be working on the computer project, just not all of you brain, your focus will be on the person in front of you. This is a kind of multitasking; just one that ties up loose ends first wherever possible.

I keep trying to remember this in my life, but every time my wife is on the phone and I ask her who is on the other end, she either ignores me or waves me off—because she is busy. I know she will get to me in a moment—I just do not like to wait.

My wife also knows I am an accomplished personal trainer who knows a lot about the muscle mechanics involved in doing exercises. Yet when she first started going to gym, and did abdominal exercises, she came back complaining of lower back pain from doing sit-ups. I made a few suggestions and waited as she continued to do the exercises in her own way up until she hurt herself. Then and only then did she ask me what exactly it was that it I had suggested.

Observe the position of your feet when you stand and walk. Most Backward Fallers tend to keep them parallel one to another. In a psychological sense, this means their energy is focused on what they are doing. There are, however, many Backward Fallers who have adapted to life's physical challenges by turning the feet outward like the other two Bio-Types. Nevertheless, the distance between the heels remains the same, and so does the tendency to focus on one thing at a time.

A Natural Observer

Your entire stance is one of observation, with the weight held naturally back over the heels. Your instincts always motivate you to observe and study first before making a decision. For example, when you meet someone new, you instinctively let that person present him or herself first. You want to hear what he has to say first. You take time to observe his clothes, mannerisms, choice of words, etc. before allowing a more personal interaction to ensue.

As a natural observer, you also like to share what you have observed with others. Your profession is most likely one where you can guide others to see things that you naturally take in, or one that includes detail-orientated tasks. Teaching, photography, journalism, production or conducting some form of therapy fit your nature.

A Few Management Tips for Dealing with Backward Fallers

Give Them Trust

If you have people working for you who are Backward Fallers, give them a clear overall goal, them let them work out and present to you the different steps they plan to follow to reach it. They tend to be independent and strong-willed, and appreciate the trust you will give them. They are usually good project managers who know how to anticipate and prevent potential problems.

Speak First

When you meet a Backward Faller, remember that this person is someone who is quite observant. In a social situation, he will wait to see how you present yourself before he takes any step. Speak first, and give him time to take in information about you, so he are is able to see whom you are, what you have to say and where you are coming from. Do not barge into a Backward Faller's space and try to get him to talk about himself when, in fact, he is the one wanting to hear about you.

Know Your Opponent

Backward Fallers follow the dictates of logic. If they believe in something, they will stand by that belief, even if it means terminating a relationship that means a lot to them. This is someone who will not let mere emotion deter them from what they have decided.

They sometimes lack physical balance. Many Backward Fallers find it hard to keep on "middle path" and will at times tend to navigate their life between extremes. They walk by pulling their body forward, using the back of their leading leg to pull themselves forward, with little or no push-off from the ball of their trailing foot. Thus, most of them never developed the strength and control in their calves to take advantage of their toes for balance. If you look at the feet of a Backward Faller, the toes do so little in the maintenance of balance that they hardly touch the floor at all Backward Fallers can ascertain how much control they still have of their toes by trying to lift alternately the big toes and then little toes separately. As the body gets older, the toes may barely touch the floor at all.

You can use certain techniques when you want to unsettle Backward Fallers:

When they rotate their body, as in to avoid a physical attack, they tend to lift one hip and are thus at risk of falling. This makes them vulnerable to sidelong attacks. In discussion with them, a question or a reference to something foreign to the matter at hand will throw them for a moment. They expect things to be presented in a straightforward, linear fashion, though non-linear private thought is common.

Force them to tell you their viewpoint first! Backward Fallers are better at listening and responding or at modifying your proposals than at taking the lead. They usually take a moment or two to consider and assess a problem before being willing to take action. They wait to hear what you have to say before they offer anything about what they are thinking.

Put pressure and force them to move first. They are much better at defending than at attacking. If threatened physically, they will wait for their opponent to move first and try to use his force against him to take him out.

Backward Fallers—Key Personality Characteristics

They deal with things in a methodical, step-by-step manner.

They are cautious and observe before moving.

Strengths

They are good planners and organizers.

They are keen observers, and foresee challenges and plan for them as much as possible before the challenges appear.

They are analytical thinkers, with strong intuitive capabilities.

Weaknesses

They are independent and strong-willed, so they want to try their own way first.

Tips for Successful Conversations

Speak first, and let them collect information about you.

Let them decide about letting you get closer in their own good time.

Be detailed and linear. Talk about the dream, but focus on the steps that will get you there.

How to Unsettle a Backward Faller

Keep changing subjects or making comments foreign to the discussion.

Force them to tell you their viewpoint first.

Put pressure on them to force them to move first.

A Few Management Tips for Dealing with Backward Fallers

Let them see clearly the overall goal you are seeking to achieve.

Use their natural organizational skills to prioritize the steps.

Let them seek out potential pitfalls and plan for them in advance.

Reminder for Other Bio-Types When Dealing With Backward Fallers

Extra Considerations if You Are a Forward Faller

Do not worry or overreact if Backward Fallers do not get as excited as you do about your dreams but rather appear to drag you down with questions about what steps you plan to take to fulfill them. Remember that their approach to life is most often linear, one thing at a time, and that they see everything as a series of steps to take.

You will do well to let go of your first reactive thoughts if the questions they are asking put you into a defensive mode. Their questions are not a rejection of your ideas. It is just them anticipating possible problems so as to help you to get what you are going for. They never even implied you would not be able to reach your goal. In fact, the opposite is true. The Backward Faller listening to you is interested enough to be looking seriously at how you will be able to achieve it.

Extra Considerations If You Are a Torso-Sway Walker

With Backward Fallers, resist the urge to ask, "What, exactly, does this have to do with me?" Do your best to put aside your own views. Educate yourself in following the step-by-step presentation of an idea, even if it seems totally outside of your own way of doing things.

Extra Considerations if You Are a Backward Faller dealing with another Backward Faller

Do not wait for another Backward Faller to start the meat of the discussion or interaction. They may well be waiting to hear what you have to say before they respond. Two Backward Fallers might make excellent ambassadors playing the let's talk about the weather and establish a rapport game, but sooner or later one of them is going to have to ask the intent of the other. So steal a page from the Torso-Sway Walker, clarify your position and compare the details as a starting point. Steal a page from the Forward Faller and put forth at least a portion of you position to get things rolling.

6

Torso-Sway Walker Bio-Types

The patterns your mind follows to achieve each goal you seek are written in the ways that your body does things naturally.

Figure 29: A Torso-Sway Walker.

You are what I call a Torso-Sway Walker. Your naturally wide stance and your strong opinions come from having to define and sometimes defend your place in this world.

You walk and stand over a wide base of support, with your feet at about shoulder-width apart. You tend to be solidly rooted both on the earth and in your opinions. You know what you believe and woe be unto the fool who tries to knock you down!

You may be strongly rooted in your ideas, but when you do make a shift in your opinions (and it often takes a long time), it is a big shift. This is because you move the entire base when you do. You may also find that you settle into a routine and like to stay there. The Torso-Sway Walker tends to be totally set where he is—until he shifts everything.

You probably excel at several things. You are the true "jack of all trades," a person of great diversity. You can be the true Renaissance person. Torso-Sway Walkers often make several dramatic career shifts in the course of their lives. You do what you do with a full heart, and a Torso-Sway Walker who is a car mechanic today might go into the field of psychology tomorrow.

As a child, you may have felt threatened or felt some reason to need this wide base of support. You may have grown up with a lot of brothers and sisters, or under a heavy burden of expectation, or possibly in a dangerous neighborhood, or with extremely intelligent parents. For whatever reason, you felt challenged and found it necessary to establish your own personality in a strong way. Your personality thus became forged in this same fire of resistance. You grew up strong, and you are strong today. You may often want to spell out for others the basis of what you believe and exactly how you see things, even if they have heard it all before.

You probably find yourself in a profession where you guide others into areas where you know the overall terrain well. You may be an agent, systems designer, advisor or specialist of some sort.

In a discussion, you wait to hear what the other person is saying before you respond. You look at an entire concept presented to you and compare it in detail to your own.

If threatened, you will hold your ground; after all, it was hard-won, and you will not give up what you have accomplished easily. However, when you do attack, you launch forward quickly—even dangerously.

When you wake up, all the warm corners of the bed will have to give up their warmth before you abandon the bed. Then you will push forward to where you see yourself next.

When you crawled as a child, you did so in a cross-lateral way, using both the right (emotional) side of your brain to move the left side of your body and the left (analytical) side of your brain to move the right side of your body in alternation. This is why you have both a creative and an analytical side to your personality.

When you were crawling, there was also a slight hesitation in the alternation between the two sides of the body. This is why there is that same hesitation among your moods, and you are either very analytical or very emotional. There is no "in-between" for you. In fact, you can be stuck in either your logic or your emotions and find it hard to switch. To create a better facility for shifting, practice touching the left knee with the right hand alternating with then the right knee with the left hand.

When you first got up to your feet as a child, you swung your legs around to the sides and forward in a kind of a four-point crawl, shifting from side-to-side. You established a walk in which you do much the same thing, and you shift your body's weight from side-to-side when you walk today.

When you bend your torso, you do so from the hips and over a wide base. When you do a full sit-up, your legs tend to be separated by about two feet, and your feet lift off the floor as your chest comes up. You are also susceptible to back injuries.

Famous Torso-Sway Walkers

Bill Clinton
David Letterman
Harvey Keitel
Joseph Stalin
Jay Leno
Al Gore
Nick Nolte

Richard Nixon
Frank Sinatra

Bill Clinton: This former president of the United States fought hard to get to his feet and establish who he became in life. As a Torso-Sway Walker, he does not back down easily from a position he takes or a goal he strives to achieve. The worst thing you can do with Torso-Sway Walkers is to attack their position head-on. The harder you push, the more firmly rooted they become—be they right or wrong. If Ken Starr and the people seeking to remove Clinton had known about Bio-Typing, they might have realized there were more effective ways to achieve their ends.

In the pictures below, we can see other determined Torso-Sway Walkers who fought hard to achieve what they wanted in life: Frank Sinatra, Sammy Davis Jr. and Richard Nixon.

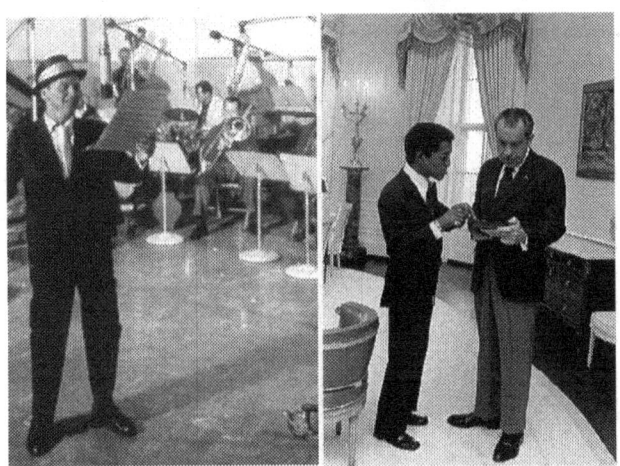 

Figure 30: Famous Torso-Sway Walkers: Frank Sinatra, Sammy Davis Jr. and Richard Nixon, and a statue depicting an ancient Roman warrior.

You can see examples of the Torso-Sway Walker clearly in ancient Roman statues. The Romans saw themselves as steadfast empire-builders who did things in their own powerful way. This is certainly not to say there were not plenty of Forward Fallers and Backward Fallers in ancient Rome. The national image that has survived in the writings and the statues seems to have glorified the Torso-Sway Walkers.

The Torso-Sway Walker Personality

Stable Base of Support

It probably took a little more time than necessary before they learned to stand and to walk upright. For some reason, they felt less supported or more vulnerable as a child than children of the other two Bio-Types. Whatever the reason, they felt the need to establish a strong, stable base of support. Maybe they had to battle to be recognized and to make their place in the world. They did so by holding onto secure physical positions. When they moved they used all four limbs, crawling fast and furiously to get to wherever they were going until the urge to discover more of the world around them and stand up became strong enough to make them change their course. When they did climb to their feet, they kept that wide, stable base and fighting spirit by establishing a strong wide, stable base of support with feet about shoulder-width apart. Do you remember my "pyramid" people?

Once they began to walk, an adjustment became necessary. In order to keep their wide base of support while moving forward, they had to shift their whole weight from one foot to the other, giving a side-to-side, ambling quality to the movement. This set in motion a specific muscular development pattern that strengthened the muscles along the sides of their body.

A Person of Strong Opinions

They take strong, sturdy physical positions and resolutely hold to their opinions and viewpoints. As children, they felt the necessity to establish vertical support in a strong way. This helped them feel better prepared to face the world. Their personality became forged in this same fire of resistance. They grew up strong, and they stayed strong. They know what they believe and anyone who tries to knock them down had better look out! If threatened, they will hold their ground. After all, it was hard-won, and they will not easily give up what they have accomplished.

Ability to Adapt

Though they may appear slow and strongly rooted in their ideas and in their life, they are open to other ways of thinking. It just takes time and patience. Given time, they are able to shift their whole body, heart and soul to new ways of being and thinking. When they make a shift, it is a big shift. This is because in the same as they face life head-on with their bodies, they also adapt to new situations by moving their entire base of thoughts, opinions and emotions. They are most likely to be comfortable in positions where they hold status. Regardless of their career choice, they can make radical changes in the course of their lives.

Live in the Present

They live in the present and want to experience the pleasures of life to their fullness before they decide to move on. For example, getting up can be a challenge if it means leaving behind the warmth of the bed, the softness of the pillow or the relaxing feeling of lying down. During the day, a natural tendency of a Torso-Sway Walker is to organize his activities according to what he most relates to at that particular time. This is most apparent when he is on a holiday, free of any professional obligations.

"No-Risk" Policy

Torso-Sway Walkers do not like to take risks. When they first learned to stand and walk, their primary concern was to maintain a strong and secure physical position. The same motivation tends to animate them today in all their undertakings. Whatever the task, they do whatsoever is necessary to remain "stable" and in control every step of the way until the task's completion, all of this in a context they understand.

Look at TV talk show hosts Jay Leno and David Letterman. They are both excellent at what they do, because they know who they are and where they are coming from. Therefore, they can be the firm anchors around which guests can be in the public's presence. Just imagine how their two long-running shows would do if these hosts could not be counted upon to be consistent!

Routines Make Life Easier

Torso-Sway Walkers may find they tend to settle into a routine and like to stay there. Change is not something they usually welcome. Torso-Sway Walkers need to have a clear picture of where and how they fit in the world and how things and people relate to them. They feel fully secure in a world they understand. As a result, they tend to be totally set where they are. To get from "here" to "there," they first have to know why and how they will do it and to what degree it fits into the plan of their life. They imagine themselves actually doing it. If a move from "here" to "there" is justified in their eyes, they will then follow a systematic path they understand.

Ability to Multitask With Full Attention

Their brain is not sequentially oriented, and they are probably comfortable doing more than one thing at a time. They naturally tend to keep their feet widely spaced and firmly rooted. This is because they are open to many things simultaneously. Whether or not they are multitasking, they always do everything with full attention. Shifting only part of their body is not a familiar feeling for them. They learned to face danger head-on and this is also how they face everything in life. They face what they are doing and give all their activities full attention. They can also excel at doing many things one at a time and can be a true "jack of all trades."

Either Creative or Analytical

When Torso-Sway Walkers crawled as a child, they did so in a unilateral way, using both the right arm and the right leg, then the left arm and the left leg. This means that they were shifting from one side of the body to the other. This also implies that similarly, they are shifting from one side of the brain to the other. It is why they have both a creative and analytical side to their personality, just not at the same time. This is why there is that same hesitation among their moods. They are either analytical or emotional and there are no "in-betweens" for them.

A Few Management Tips for Dealing with Torso-Sway Walkers

Find Common Ground

The key to effective communication with Torso-Sway Walkers is finding a point of common experience between you upon which to build a foundation. Remember that simply by the way you present yourself, they are going to look at you from their place in the world, then decide if you fit into it or not.

Let Them Speak. You Listen

When you meet a Torso-Sway Walker, give them time to present themselves fully and establish who they are. They need to figure out if they are going to allow you to fit into their world. If you press your agenda before understanding what they want you to know about them, you will not be able to interact successfully. Remain patient as they weave their world in front of you. By giving them the time to approach you regarding any business or communication, you create a safe space in which to interact with them.

A Rock Has Many Qualities

Torso-Sway Walkers stand by the beliefs and traditions of their organization. They are great individuals to choose when you want someone who has strong character and nerves or who can take a strong stand at the negotiating table. They solidly hold to whatever position they have and still have the ability to swing 180 degrees if the need arises.

Know Your Opponent

Because the toes and the balls of their feet bear only a small portion of the weight of their body, the muscles in their calves that control the movements of the ankles are weak. As a result, they tend to lack balance and fluidity in their movements as well as lack balance and fluidity in their personal life. Many Torso-Sway Walkers find it hard to stay on "the middle path," and they sometimes may navigate their life between extremes.

You can develop the following techniques when you want to unsettle Torso-Sway Walkers:

A question or a reference to something foreign or out of context to a matter under discussion will throw them for a moment. When pushed off-balance, Torso-Sway Walkers shift their body laterally to compensate and regain balance. This is an unusual position for them. Get them off balance mentally, and they will be vulnerable. This can be good if it allows you to present new things to them. It can be bad if they feel too vulnerable and close off.

Torso-Sway Walkers—Key Personality Characteristics

They have strong opinions and they are firmly rooted to the earth.

Strengths

They have strength of character, with a solid belief system.

They are strong advocates.

Weaknesses

They do not accept change easily.

Tips for Successful Conversations

Let Them Speak First. You Listen.

Find common ground; show them how you fit into their world before presenting your ideas.

How to Unsettle a Torso-Sway Walker

Tell them you have your own way of doing things, and you expect them to accept and apply it without questions.

A Few Management Tips for Dealing with Torso-Sway Walkers

Make sure they see the purpose of the tasks you put before them.

Take the time to be sure they are aligned with you in the goals.

Let them tell you their considerations, and try to see their viewpoint as well as your own.

Reminder for Other Bio-Types in Dealing With Torso-Sway Walkers

Extra Considerations If You Are a Forward Faller

Keep close focus on the "here and now." Torso-Sway Walkers are put off by people whose heads are in the fulfillment of the dream and are losing sight of their current foundation. Where they are right now is important to Torso-Sway Walkers, and giving up all of that security for something unknown may be unacceptable to them.

Extra Considerations if You Are a Backward Faller

When you interact with Torso-Sway Walkers, make sure to include something they can relate to. They do not like to hear intellectual, step-by-step descriptions of a given project—even less so if it's got nothing to do with them. If they do listen, they are probably doing it with reluctance. Find common ground first. Let them tell you where they are coming from, and align your presentation to their stated beliefs.

Extra Considerations if You Are a Torso-Sway Walker Dealing with Another Torso-Sway Walker

First, be sure and ask to hear their position before you offer your own. This will put the Torso-Sway Walker on firm ground, familiar ground. Learn to wait to let the Torso-Sway Walker tell you all about where they personally are coming from. You can even compare points of similarity and difference without needing to say anything first. Learn from the Forward Faller to picture and describe a clear goal. Learn from the Backward Faller to consider out loud the steps necessary to reach that goal.

7

Reading Other People

Each system in the human body seems to have a parallel with what we learn in other areas of our lives. The digestive and excretory systems teach us to accept and take in some things while letting go of others. Our physical balance system helps us find emotional and intellectual balance. The sense of sight teaches us to perceive, organize and recognize what is around us.

All of this self-examination has led you to begin to see how different we really are from one other. Now that we have looked at ourselves in a new way, let us begin to look at other people.

Once we become proficient in Bio-Typing ourselves, we can begin to apply all the new stuff we are seeing in ourselves to our interactions with the other people in our world.

Back to My Experiences…

One of the most distressing things about autism is that my mind works so differently from the way other people's minds work. Throughout my life, I seldom knew how others were going to react to most of the things I would say or do.

Approaching someone at a social function and starting a conversation could be very trying, and not just for me, because I might very well say whatever popped into my head. You see, I knew I did not share a common mental context with others and could not read their faces, so I had to find some other way of anticipating how they were going to interact with me. Like a good general going into battle, I had to learn how to read people before I "attacked." All too often, the person I was approaching would indeed feel attacked when I was not careful in my method of approach.

If you find the need to call up a store to discuss returning something you bought to get your money back, you probably have a good idea of what to say and how the person you are talking to will respond. In the same position, I have had no idea how to handle it. I expected either anger or total disinterest in anything I might have to say. I would be so totally at a loss in this kind of situation that I would just rather lose the money.

As I have explained, I had to learn to look at people from the outside and extrapolate from how they did things physically what would be the best methods of approaching and interacting with them. What I was able to learn about bodies even taught me to deal with the disembodied voices on the telephone.

With the Bio-Typing information in this book, you can use what I figured out without having to figure out each personality for yourself. You can simply Bio-Type people, apply my way of handling them in your own interactions, and see for yourself if it works for you. I think you will find that it does. Like me, you can learn how best to approach people you have not met yet without being "hit." If you can determine a person's Bio-Type, you have won more than half the battle.

The key to seeing other people is knowing what to look for and where to look for it. The clothes they are wearing are what they want you to look at. Bio-Typing tells you much more.

In the self-diagnostic chapter, you had a chance to look at yourself, see how your body naturally does things and figure out your own Bio-Type. When you read the description of your own Bio-Type and that of others, you found much that could be known about you and the people in your life. Now let us take it "on the road" and begin to observe other people in this new way.

They Won't Bio-Type Themselves for You

Since you cannot very well ask a stranger to go Bio-Type himself and report back to you, let's try seeing if we can start to Bio-Type other people.

Bio-Typing Practice at Home

Before you even go out into the street, use the TV to practice Bio-Typing. It is filled with examples of things you always look at but have maybe never really "seen." Watch people who's Bio-Type you already know. For instance, if you happen to see footage of George W. Bush, you can see that he is a Backward

Faller. Notice his parallel feet and the way he pulls himself forward with each step. See how his weight is over his heels. He is someone that keeps pulling himself step-by step toward his goals.

Figure 31: Tom Ridge (left) Torso-Sway Walker—George W. Bush (right)
Backward Faller

Spend an hour or two with Jay Leno or David Letterman. These Torso-Sway Walkers are prime examples of widely spread feet. The two men have a clear idea of where they are coming from.

Watch the Discovery Channel. It is filled with Forward Fallers out having adventures, mixed in with some Backward Fallers explaining things.

Figure 32: Examples of famous members of each of the Bio-Types, John
F. Kennedy, Forward Faller, Frank Sinatra, Torso-Sway Walker, and two
Backward Fallers, Ronald Reagan and Margaret Thatcher.

These Forward Fallers tend to go off trying to do things that have never been
done before. They have a vision and figure out how to make it real as they go.
You already know a lot about looking at foot position in relation to centerlines,

and the various muscles that are used for common actions such as balance and breathing.

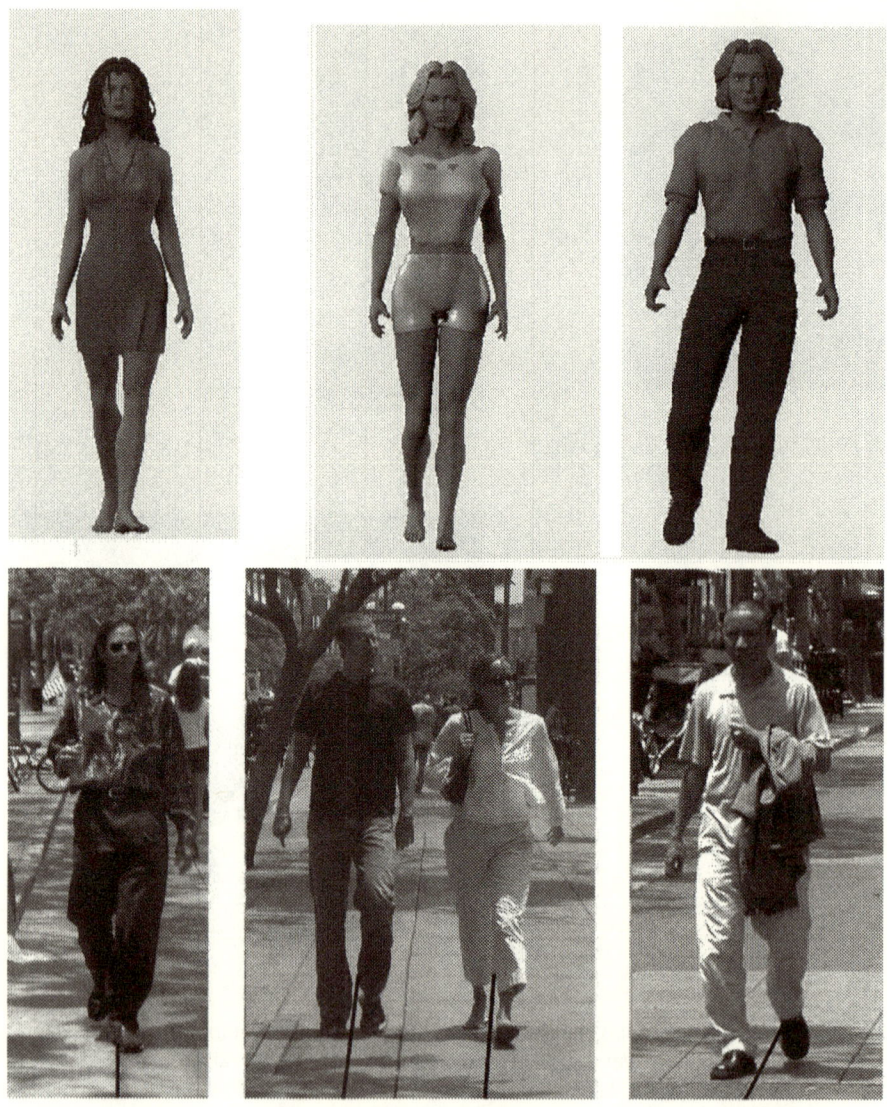

Figure 33: A Forward Faller (left), Two Backward Fallers (center), A Torso-Sway Walker (right).

Once you spot someone's Bio-Type, refer back to either Chapter 4 (Forward Fallers), Chapter 5 (Backward Fallers) or Chapter 6 (Torso-Sway Walkers). Go for it! In no time at all, you will easily remember all of it.

Let's Start Looking at Other People

Now we are going to start looking at people to learn what to look at and what to look for. When looking to see how others do things, always remember to refer back to how your own body does things. Try moving or holding your own body, the way the person you are observing moves or holds his.

Remember, it took me a little time to be able to read Bio-Types, so start simple. Find a public place where people congregate, such waiting for a bus or movie. Look at the differences in the positions of their feet. Some will have their heels two to four inches apart, the heels of others will be touching, and still others will have their heels shoulder-width apart. Some will have their feet turned outward. Some will have their feet parallel.

Just pretend you lost a contact lens, and look at the ground and people's feet. However you do it, start looking at people's feet and seeing, perhaps for the first time, that the feet tell a lot about a person—not the shoes!

Remember, for right now we are just looking at the distance between a person's heels when that person is standing naturally. Besides the fact that there are different distances between feet, some are parallel, and others turned outward, we are going to begin to discover what I call the "base of support" of different people.

Discovering a Person's Base of Support

The first thing I always look at is the base upon which individuals are standing. I identify people as having either a wide base with a substantial distance between the heels, or a narrower base with only a little distance between the heels, or a tight base with heels right under their center of gravity. If you look at people in this way, you will see that when they walk, they just naturally move over that base. They walk with more or less distance between their feet.

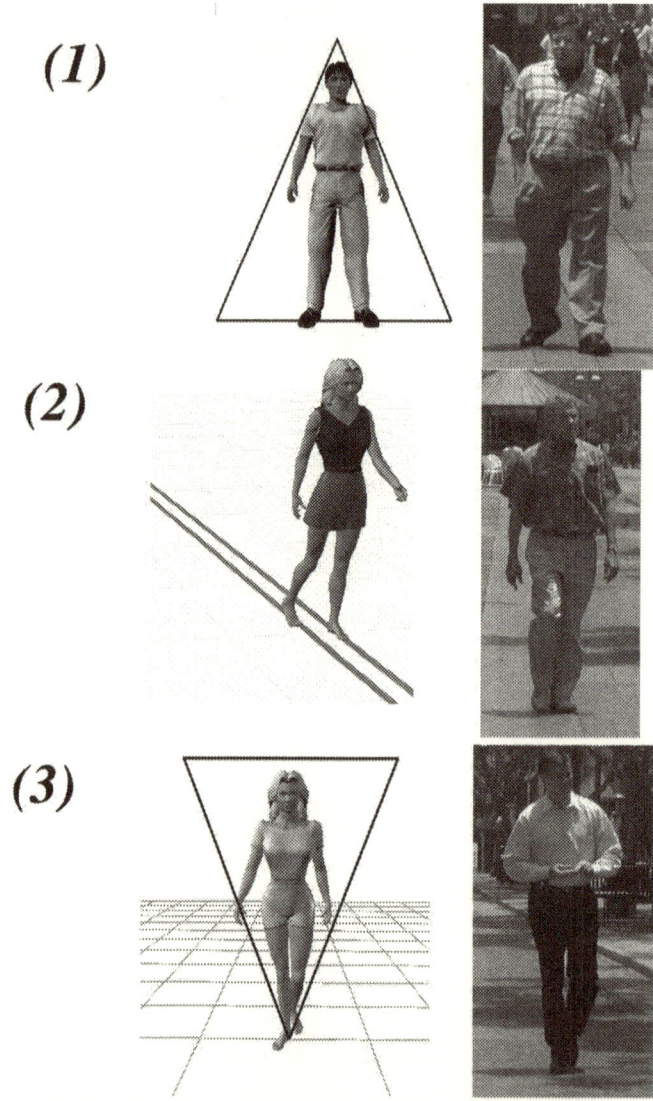

Figure 34: A pyramid base, a railroad base and an inverted pyramid base.

To me, they are something like pyramids gliding down the street (figure 34, #1), or they are like freight trains moving down tracks (figure 34, #2), or they are like inverted pyramids standing over heels that touch (figure 34, #3).

You have never seen a pyramid gliding down the street or a set of train tracks under a person? Well, neither have I. Nevertheless, if you see a bunch of people standing around in a circle at a class or in a group watching something, just look at their feet and imagine the rest. You will always see that some of them have their feet turned outward with their heels set wide apart, or their heels are slightly apart, either parallel or slightly turned outward. The feet of Backward Fallers are slightly separated, usually parallel but sometimes turned outward. Forward Fallers have their toes turned out and heels touching. Torso-Sway Walkers have their feet turned out and shoulder-width apart. When you are looking at any bunch of people, you are always looking at a bunch of Bio-Types. When they walk, they are showing you their Bio-Types, too, but then you have to catch it as they move!

Remember, in observing other people, what we are looking for first is the distance between their heels! Look at figure 35. What do you see?

Figure 35: Three Bio-Types Walking

Unless you need to make a proposal to your boss today or figure out how best to deal with your spouse in the next 10 minutes, go to the mall and get busy observing. You can also go back to your TV and look at people to practice your observing skills.

Look Under the Feet!

Next, we are going to look at where the feet fall when people walk. This is best done in relation to a centerline, but to do this, of course, you need to have one. There will be things you can use as centerlines all over the place, e.g., lines on the sidewalk, etc. If you do not have a handy centerline, just close one eye and watch the space (or lack of it) between people's feet as they walk, and the side-to-side movement of their heads.

If the observed person has his falling feet on either side of the centerline, or if there is just a little space between them, then you are probably looking at a Backward Faller. The Backward Faller's head will move a little bit side-to-side. Backward Fallers walk with their feet landing on either side of their center of gravity or the centerline, so their heads naturally move. There are many Backward Fallers in the news or entertainment industry demonstrating this for you every day. Oprah Winfrey is an example. Remember, the feet can be either parallel or slightly turned outward. I always think of these people as railroad trains moving along their appointed tracks.

In cities, Backward Fallers are the most common Bio-Type. This is because the kinds of jobs that people do there require observation and clarification for others. There are likely to be many teachers, journalists, accountants, and production people in cities.

If the person you are observing has his or her heels landing on a centerline or falling in front of each other and they are turned outward, you have probably found a Forward Faller. Watch for movement of the head as he walks. Do their heads remain perfectly centered, not moving side-to-side at all? Because Forward Fallers place their feet directly under their center of gravity when they walk, there is no lateral movement of the head. Find a movie with Robert Downey Jr. in it or with Timothy Dalton. Watch them walk toward the camera and see how there is no lateral movement of their head. Forward Fallers live in cities, but usually in smaller numbers. They are the ones that are advancing new concepts and designing projects from the inception stage.

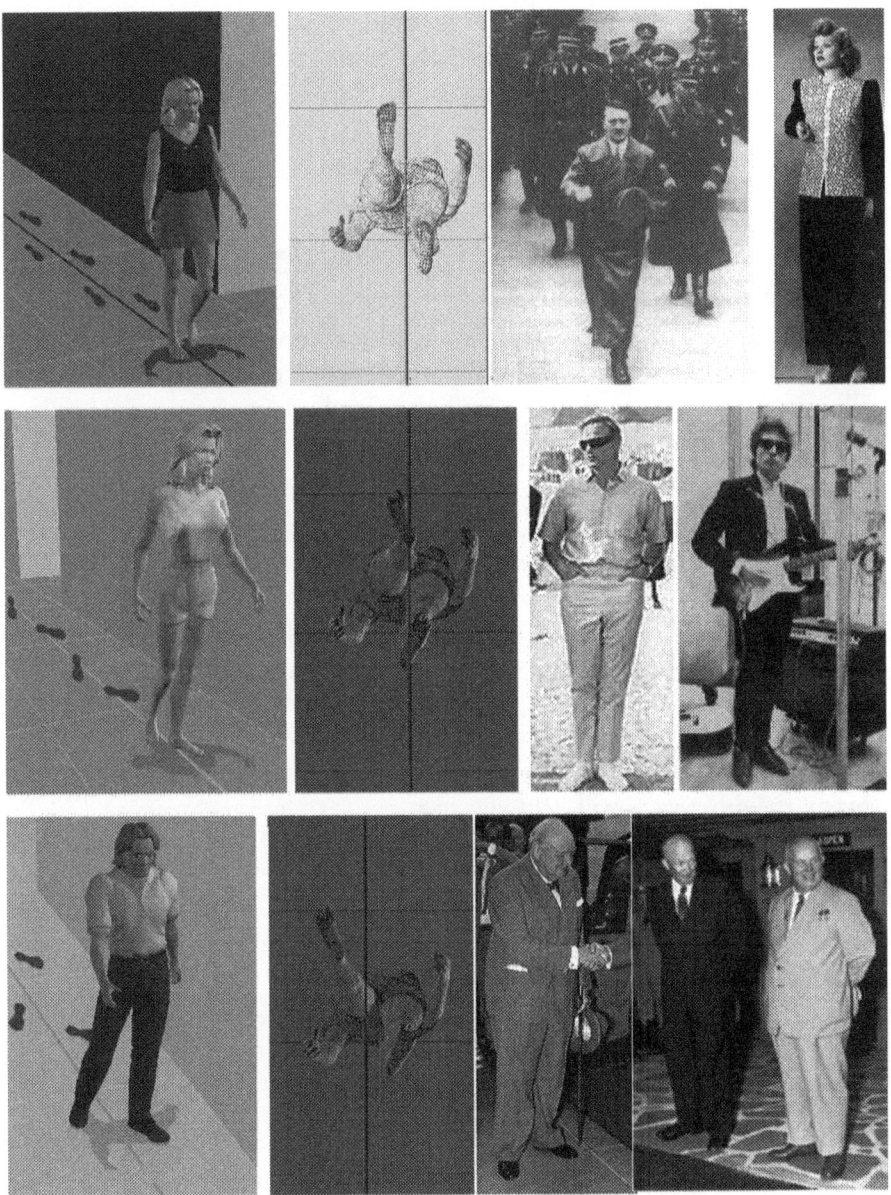

Figure 36: (1) Backward Fallers, (2) Forward Fallers, (3) Torso-Sway
Walkers

If the person you are observing has his feet landing six to twelve inches apart, and
turned outward, then you may have yourself a Torso-Sway Walker. Watch the

side-to-side movements of the head as he walks. The Torso-Sway Walker's head will move a lot from side-to-side. This wide base of support necessitates a lateral movement of the head. Look at Jay or David. Torso-Sway Walkers can be found anywhere, but wherever you find them, they will always be pyramid-like in their stature, either standing firmly over a wide base or shifting dramatically from side-to-side as they walk.

If you find it difficult to tell whether the head is moving laterally, try this: Close one eye, and look at something behind the person as he walks. If his head is moving from side-to-side, it will alternately block and reveal the object behind the walker. I admit this will take a little bit of practice to identify, but what is it worth to you to know in advance how best to understand and to relate to someone you do not know yet?

Further Verifications of Bio-Types

Next, we want to use the other tests to verify our first impression. If you can simply ask the people you are observing to take a deep breath or stand on one foot and balance, go for it. Often this may not be possible (even though you might really enjoy seeing your boss standing on one foot holding his or her breath!).

There are things you can look at that will verify for you if your first assessment is right. You can also observe people from the side. This is a little more difficult, but picturing the differences will help you picture the difference from one Bio-Type to the next more easily.

From the side, look at where their weight is held over the arch of their feet. Forward Fallers hold their weight more forward over the balls of the feet. Backward Fallers and Torso-Sway Walkers hold their weight more over their heels. If a person's weight is toward the heels, look next at the distance between his feet.

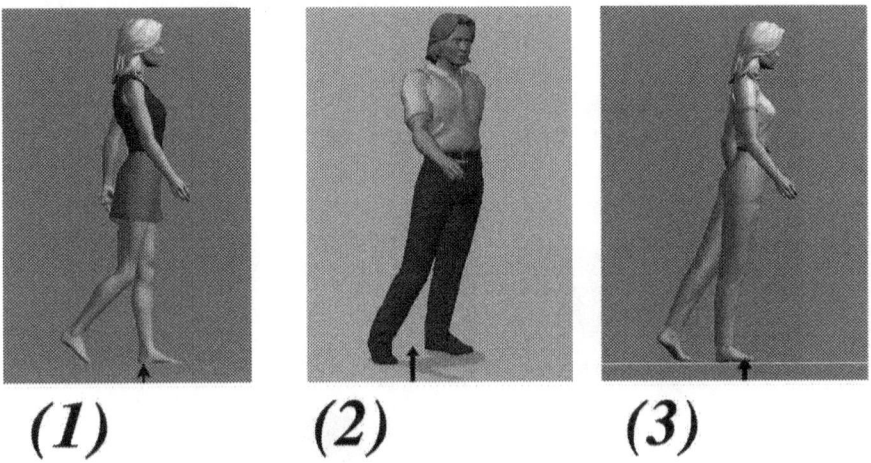

(1)   **(2)**   **(3)**

Figure 37: (1) Backward Faller, (2) Torso-Sway Walker, (3) Forward
Faller.

People often bend over when they are out in public, and we must be ready to watch closely how they do it. When people are not bowing, I watch them bend their bodies as they sit down or pick things up. I do drop things a lot, and sometimes this does the trick.

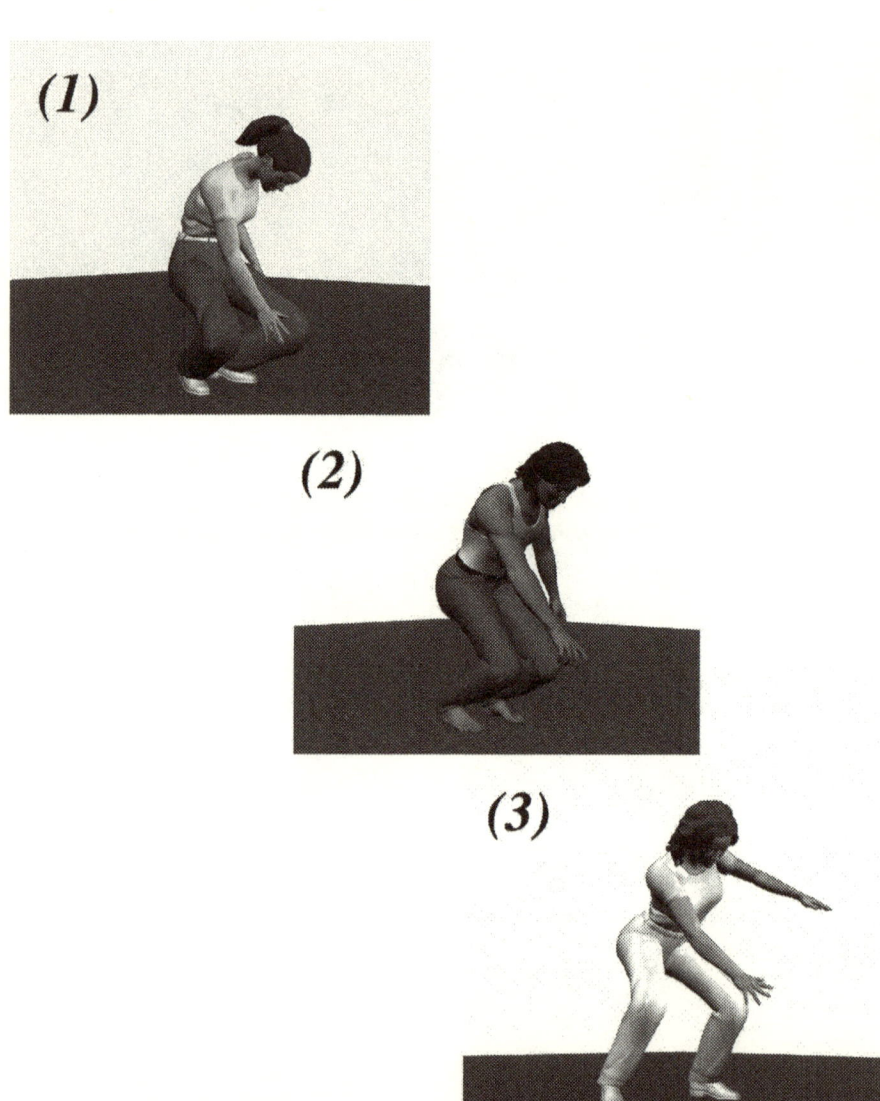

Figure 38: (1) Forward Faller, (2) Backward Faller, (3) Torso-Sway
Walker.

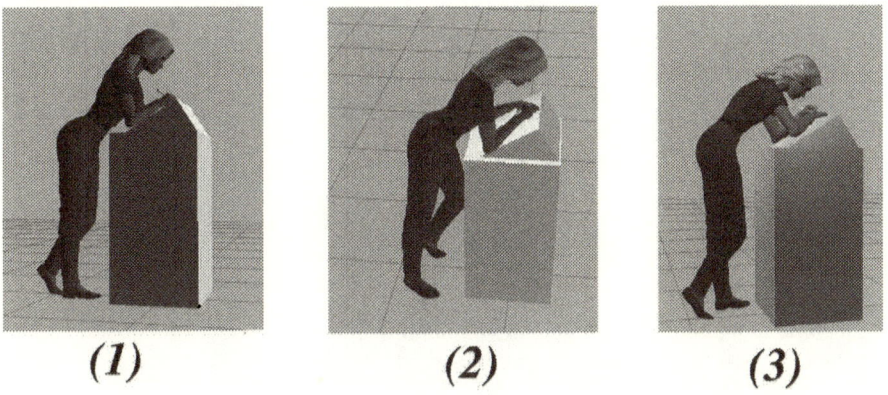

Figure 39: (1) Backward Faller, (2) Torso-Sway Walker, (3) Forward
Faller.

Now if we could just get them to take a deep breath, we could observe which muscle actions they use most for breathing. When I tell a really bad joke, I often get people to take a deep breath and let it out. What we want to look at in either case is what moves when they breathe.

Backward Fallers lift the chest by arching the back when they breathe. Forward Fallers fill their bellies and do not arch the back. Torso-Sway Walkers spread the chest to the sides when they breathe.

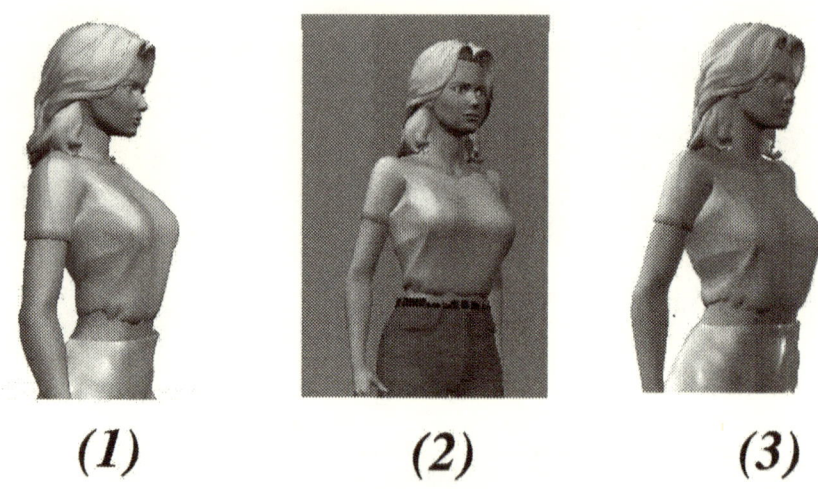

(1)   *(2)*   *(3)*

Figure 40: (1) Backward Faller, (2) Forward Faller, (3) Torso-Sway
Walker.

Again, the balance test is a little difficult to do with a stranger who is not aware
you are Bio-Typing him. If "stepping on his toes" seems inappropriate, skip this
one. You probably have already gotten all the verification you need.

By now, you probably have realized that just by stopping and looking around,
you cannot help but see that everybody falls perfectly into one of the three Bio-
Types.

Figure 41: (1) Torso-Sway Walkers, (2) Backward Fallers, (3) Forward Fallers.

My wife and I once traveled down a river in the Ecuadorian Amazon in a 40 foot dugout canoe. We had been traveling for 10 days, making our way towards the border of Peru to find a Jaguar shaman we had heard about named Mengatui. I was just starting to write this book, and I was curious t find out whether my idea would crossover into his culture. What if the three Bio-Types were found only in developed countries?

What made me begin to think about this was the way that monkeys walk with their backs arched and their weight over their heels. Maybe people simply adapted to the landscape of their environment as animals did. Because there are no sidewalks in the jungle, maybe the indigenous people were of a different Bio-

Type that I had never seen before, or maybe they all walked like Backward Fallers.

As we were getting out of the boat on the day of our arrival at the shaman's village, we noticed three hunters walking over to greet us. They were carrying some spider monkeys from the hunt. The men were laughing and talking loudly, and what I saw blew me away. The first was a Torso-Sway Walker, the next was a Forward Faller, and the third was a Backward Faller!

In all the years since I began sharing my way of looking at people with others, neither I nor anyone else I have taught it to has come across anyone who was not one of the three Bio-Types.

The Conversation Test: Listening to What People Say and How They Context Things

If all else fails, and you cannot get the person to stand up, walk or do anything physical, you can try to talk to them. The way they go about telling you about things will tell you their Bio-Type as well.

Imagine you just asked someone for directions.

The Backward Faller will give you directions in a step-by-step manner, just as he walks. "All right, you need to get to the corner of such-and-such, walk to the next corner, turn left, walk three blocks, and then you…"

The Torso-Sway Walker will first tell you where you are now, then give you directions to where you want to go—just the way he is concerned with where he himself is coming from in life. "Well, right now you are at the southeast corner of such-and-such, and if you want to get to…"

The Forward Faller will focus on where you are going and skip a lot of what will seem to him as unnecessary detail. After all, it is about where you want to go. "The library? That's at Broadway and Main." The Forward Faller pictures what getting there will look like, and then figures out what is needed to get there.

You can turn all this around if you need to give them directions.

The Backward Faller will want things presented to him in a step-by-step, process-oriented manner.

The Torso-Sway Walker will understand and remember better if you begin by telling him where he is right now and how you usually get to the same place he is trying to get to.

The Forward Faller will want you to focus on where he wants to go. Give him the overall picture (main streets), and skip the little details (small streets).

There is always a way to determine someone's Bio-Type, from initial impressions of others walking either toward us, away from us or past us, and even from careful listening to him. Chapters 4, 5 and 6 gave you insights into the personality of each Bio-Type. Chapters 8, 9 and 10 cover how to apply this new knowledge to love, friendship and all of your personal and business relationships.

8

Applying Bio-Typing: Love & Friendships

The human being's capacity for seeing only what he expects to see is surpassed only by his ability to expect others to understand things the way he does. Thus, it sometimes seems that true communication can happen only between like-minded individuals. No wonder the world is a mess! We really need to start learning to listen to people who think differently and to embrace our differences.

Here, for me, is what this whole book is really about: how I have been able to use what I read in a person's Bio-Type to make interpersonal communication possible for me and how you can use Bio-Typing to make interpersonal relations dramatically better for you.

When you are able to distinguish the differences between yourself and others in fundamental things like how they take in information and how they resolve problems in all areas of their lives, you can enjoy a new clarity when relating with them. Now you can use that knowledge to shift your view of the world to dovetail with theirs. You can know in advance the best way to approach and communicate with any person you encounter, in the first seconds you are with him.

You might think of it like using astrology, only better. Knowing a person's astrological sign may give you some clues as to what he may be like, things to look out for or information about tendencies common to people of his sign. Knowing people's Bio-Type gives you a lot more specific information about how they see themselves in relation to their world, written in a lifetime's use of their body and deciphered in the ways they do things physically. If you can see how they approach and execute activities such as standing, walking, breathing, etc. and how they take in information, you can predict how they are going to take in what you say and how they will approach the ideas or opportunities that you are presenting.

Fortunately, there are only so many possible patterns of usage in the musculature; namely, three. With astrology, you have 12 possible sun signs and a person's rising sign to further complicate the situation. Bio-Typing is much simpler. With Bio-Typing, there are only three possibilities, and every single person you meet is going to fall into one of them perfectly.

With practice, the "rules of engagement" with Bio-Types are going to work for every single individual in each group, every single time. If we are talking to a "pyramid," (Torso-Sway Walker) we need to remember that "pyramids" are powerfully rooted to where they see themselves coming from and their sense of who they are. Remember that turning a Torso-Sway Walker to face your point of view can be a lot more work than you might anticipate. So remember what they say about teaching pigs to fly: It irritates the pig and frustrates the teacher! Look for common ground or common experiences, and build upon them in your communications with Torso-Sway Walkers.

If you are dealing with a "freight train," (Backward Faller) look at the track he is on, and decide where he is headed and where you want him to go. Then wait until either you find a rail-switcher along his path or he stops to rest. I will never get anywhere with my Backward Faller wife if I try to derail her from her own logic to impose my own. I need to let her get to asking me what I see before I blurt out what I think she needs to know. If you are interacting with an "inverted pyramid," (Forward Faller) show him a well-embellished well-described place to land, and get out of his way.

On top of this, if you are a neurotypical (normal) person, you have the advantage of not having either the face blindness or the mind blindness that made it necessary for me to devise this system in the first place.

The Different Bio-Types in Relationships

When individuals of different Bio-Types are in a relationship, often they can find it difficult to understand how the differences in their Bio-Types come into play in nearly every area of their lives together. I know that often my best friend's way of looking at things can really puzzle me. After all, if I see things so clearly in my way, why doesn't she see them in the same way?

One of the truly wonderful things in personal relationships is that we are so different from each other, and two heads are better than one—if they provide a broader perspective on things rather than misunderstandings.

When we express our dreams and plans to our best allies, they can seem to be shooting holes in our sails, when in fact, they are only trying to help us in the best way they know how.

Forward Fallers see success in the clarity of the vision. One of their complaints may be, "When I tell her about my dreams, my friend slams me with all the things that can go wrong! Why can't she just share my dream with me? By the time she's done finding things that can go wrong, I just want to give up and not even try."

Forward Fallers can innovate, lead the way and allow Backward Fallers to do what they do best: foresee obstacles and figure out strategies. Torso-Sway walkers can provide the stability that keeps Forward Fallers from getting too far out on a limb. Backward Fallers can help Torso-Sway walkers take the steps involved in shifting gears and trying new things. We chose certain people that are intrinsically different from us in forming our relationships.

Backward Fallers see success in the individual steps leading toward a goal. One of their complaints may be, "Why can't my friend see that I want so badly for her to get where she wants to go that I try to think of everything she's going to need to do in order to win?"

Torso-Sway Walkers see success in the continuity of the dreamer and the dream. One of their complaints may be "It all sounds really interesting, but what has this project got to do with my life as it is today?"

Where one Bio-Type focuses on the result and will deal with any problem along the way with all the energy and enthusiasm necessary (Forward Faller), another tries to concentrate on all details because this is the best way he knows to support his beloved (Backward Faller). Yet another is so concerned with maintaining the things that he has attained thus far in life that he does not understand the need to change (Torso-Sway Walker).

You can learn to analyze the individuals in your everyday life and learn to understand how it is that what might look like an argument or "raining on your parade" is really just a basic difference in perspectives.

Have you ever heard the story of the three blind men describing an elephant? They were each examining it with their hands. One man was feeling the trunk, another was feeling the side, and the third was feeling the tail. Not surprisingly, each one described what he thought an elephant was in very different terms!

This book can teach you to use a completely new way of looking at people in order to help you to understand what they feel when they "touch the elephant" or when they discuss their dreams with you. You can learn to understand where they are coming from and learn great new ways to dramatically improve your relationships with them. You will be able to respond to their actual perception of things, rather than to their reaction as interpreted by your way of seeing things.

We often hear people say things such as, "Try to see this from my point of view." Now you really can!

Remember, an individual's personality today is based upon how he first approached everyone and everything in his world as a child. If he continually felt he needed to define and defend himself, he might now feel as if he needs to defend himself from you. The patterns of relating and interacting began for people when they were first beginning to experience people and things outside of themselves.

The knowledge that Bio-Typing imparts paves the road to a broader, richer dimension of personal relationships. If we can recognize that different people think differently and take in information differently, we can begin to interact in accordance with these differences.

Communication Between Spouses

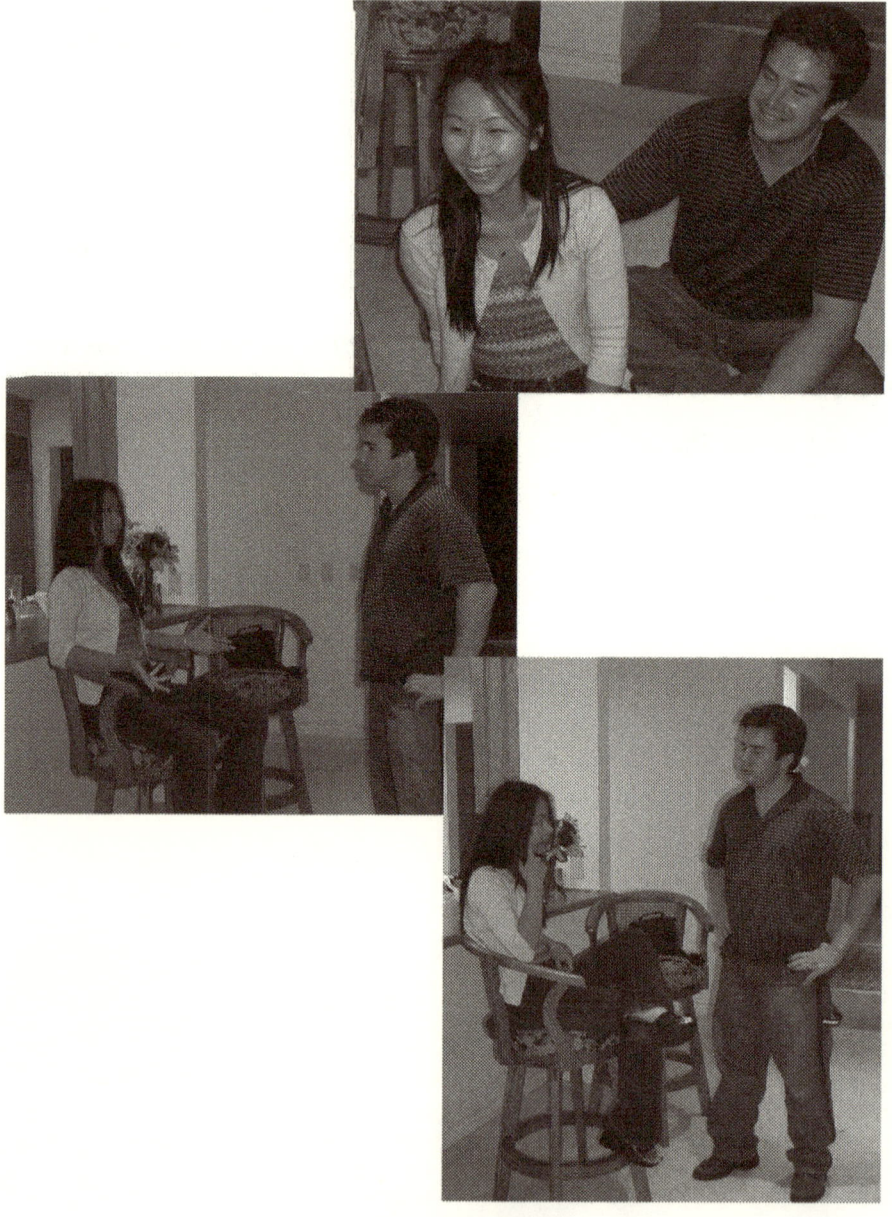

Figure 42: Really seeing your loved ones requires looking at them with a new set of eyes.

Remember in the earlier section on the "theory of mind" I recounted how I was always somewhat different from others? Neurotypical people assume that they share a basic understanding of how each other's heads work because they all share a similar social upbringing. Just how does it come to be assumed that they share the same innate ability to know certain "rules of engagement" for social interactions? I am here to tell you: They do not!

At home, it helps to understand and speak the language of your spouse. I know that during the early years of my marriage Chris, my wife, was often at a loss when trying to figure me out. Aside from such little things as my rocking myself to sleep in bed every night, she also had to deal with my simply presuming that she knew exactly what was going on in my head at any given moment.

I would typically start a conversation saying something like, "Do you think he will like the red one?" To which she might well respond, "Do I think who will like the red what?" She had to learn to patiently ask me who and what was I talking about.

In a similar way, each Bio-Type thinks that the other two Bio-Types perceive and solve problems exactly the way they do. None of the three can conceive of anyone "normal" doing anything differently than they would. If this seems preposterous, ask someone how all people walk. He will show you how he walks. Of course, his way is the normal way to walk. How else could anyone walk? Well, the Backward Faller pulls himself forward step-by-step, the Forward Faller advances the weight over the ball of the foot and falls forward, and the Torso-Sway Walker shifts the weight to one side and swings a leg around and forward, pulling himself onto it.

What we have here can be compared to the Tower of Babel. A bunch of the ancients sought to build a tower so tall, it would reach heaven. God caused them all to begin speaking to each other in different languages, bringing the project to a halt. Here we are in a place of misunderstanding based upon the belief that everyone else is like us, sees things as we do, and should understand us because we understand ourselves—at least, we think we do.

Think of three different people considering a high-rise building they want to build together. The Forward Faller is focused on what the world below will look like from the top of this building, how far he will be able to see. The Torso-Sway Walker is focused on the foundation upon which the building will be built, whether or not it is broad enough or deep enough. The Backward Faller, on the other hand, is concerned about how each successive floor will be built, one upon the other.

All Bio-Types expect information to be presented to them in the way that they themselves might present it. Understanding the differences in each other's communication style, you can now have the ability to shift your presentation to fit their way of listening, thereby preventing unnecessary frustration and conflict. Believe me; I know about frustration and conflict!

When I think back to crouching in that bed, in that dormitory, in that long-ago summer camp that my parents put me in, it is as fresh and real as the chair I am sitting in right now. I can still feel the distant rumbling of voices in the background at that moment I knew there were the other children around me. I realize today that I must have presented quite a scene of strangeness to them. What a sight! Looking at this strange-looking kid banging his head against the brass headboard must have looked ridiculous to them and generated their nervous laughter. Yet I am sure every one of those kids had his own moments of aloneness, separateness and terror. Laughter is the spasmodic release of tension that builds up in imagining something is happening to us. The reaction of the other children was just as natural to them as banging my head was to me.

If they had been able to feel my thoughts, they probably would have reacted differently, but I also know they really would have liked to be able to understand someone who was different from them. It is human nature to want to understand other people. All it really takes is looking at ourselves and seeing our best efforts at being human as compared to someone else's best efforts to do so, too. Accepting that there are differences between us is a wonderful thing!

I am writing this book in the hopes that it will open the way to seeing each other more clearly and appreciating each other more.

Let us begin to examine the best ways to interact with others in social situations.

Bio-Typing Applied to Social Situations

The single most valuable thing I think I have been able to share with anyone about his or her own personal interactions, is something I learned in my own relationships. I have learned to ask myself when I am upset with someone, "Exactly what is it that I want this person to really hear from me, and how do I want this person to respond?" Once I establish this, I can figure out how I would have to rephrase what it is I want to say in order to have the person really understand it and to respond as I want him to respond.

Then I can decide whether or not I am willing to do or say what is necessary. It really helps to stop to take stock of the way I naturally go about saying and doing things and decide if my natural way is really the best way in this circumstance. Then I can reorganize both sides of this communication, taking into account the other person's Bio-Type.

Learn to see and relate to the little child that became the full-grown person in front of you, not to the costume he wears or the role in life that he is playing. In many ways, an individual's personality is based upon how he approaches everything and everyone in his world. This complex of characteristics did not appear on his 21st birthday. It all started as a toddler trying to get up and walk, taking on the conquest of gravity and the secrets of locomotion. How he solved these early challenges established the basis of his problem-assessment and problem-solving mechanisms. He may have spent a lifetime perfecting them, but the core features never changed. The child he was shaped the adult he is today—or soon will be.

Knowing how to best approach people also gives you the confidence to strike up conversations with strangers you might have otherwise found completely unapproachable—without finding your foot in your mouth!

Dealing with Backward Fallers

The more observant, more careful children used more of their back postural support muscles in order to lift their head higher and get a bigger picture of the world ahead of them before moving toward something that interested them. When these individuals succeeded in getting up, they did so independently and without external support. Then they began the process of pulling themselves forward, one determined step at a time, to reach what they were observing. They probably still approach new things and new people in the same way, observing carefully first, taking in all the information they can and then going forward in an orderly step-by-step manner.

If you find yourself approaching a person and you would like to get to know him or her, check out if they maintain the weight of their body back over their heels, with feet parallel and about two inches apart. If so, then you know they are a Backward Faller. You can expect he will be someone who is extremely observant and consequently aware of his surroundings. This individual is going to observe and decide how to relate with you do based upon that examination and how you present yourself to him, taking things sequentially and building a coherent picture. In a social situation, he will wait to see how you present yourself before he takes any step further. You will want to give him the time to take in information about you, so he is able to see who you are, what you have to say and where you are coming from. So talk; tell him the things he needs to know to get a firm handle on you. Do not try to get a Backward Faller to talk about himself when he is the one waiting to hear about you so he can make the decision on whether or not to become involved with you.

If he seems to be dissecting the viability of an idea you present, it is not that they do not love or trust you; it is just that he always has done things on his own, taking full responsibility for making them work. He wants to give you and your idea the same best shot at working out. He has always learned for himself. In fact, probably his strong, independent nature first drew you to him.

If he seems to get his jollies by pointing out all the things that could go wrong or all the details that haven't even come up yet, it is only because he has a naturally one-step-at-a-time approach to life. Remember that he is a person that got to his feet independently of any external support. Just watch the way he walks, pulling himself forward one-step after another.

In fact, let him run with the details. He is good at it. Just sit there and listen as he goes over the steps in his process.

Backward Fallers are naturally observant, constantly taking in all the facts before making decisions. Do not forget that Backward Fallers are also very independent. "Thank you, but I'll do it for myself" might well be their theme song. Their dominant back postural support muscles were developed in the process of raising their head as high as possible as early as possible, to see as much as possible of what was going on around them. From the earliest point in childhood, these individuals made decisions based upon observations and not without careful assessment of the facts.

My wife is a Backward Faller. When she is doing something on the computer and runs into a problem, my first instinct as a Forward Faller is to want to fix quickly it. Naturally, I want to just rush in, take over and show her what she should do. Wrong! If you see a freight train going on the wrong track, you don't get in the way to redirect it, do you? The same rule applies with Backward Fallers. They are moving along a track, and you need to wait patiently until they come to a snag or a point of indecision. Only at this point, will a gentle suggestion land upon fertile ground. When you learn to redirect gently them in a way that does not derail them, they will see your point, even if they fail to give you credit for the help.

Do not burst upon them and try pushing them "off their tracks." Derailed trains often land on innocent bystanders. Instead, I have learned that with Backward Fallers, the best thing I can do is get them to go over for me what they would do and what they envision as the best route. Let them validate their reputation as great producers, planners and directors. This validates them, and then you can ask them if they have tried this or that, allowing them to realign themselves in some direction you see as working better.

In other words, do not step into their path. Do not contradict them. Backward Fallers tend to argue the correctness of their actions with a violence that matches your carelessness in wading into their process. Give them validation of their viewpoint first to defuse possible conflict, and then provide them with the information that you or someone else should have provided earlier, and let them reorient their process toward success.

Above all, let them credit themselves with success. If you want to see if this is a good idea, just say something like, "Well, thank God I came to your rescue!" Then run!

Dealing with Forward Fallers

These more precocious children used a lot more of the muscles along the front of their body. You can clearly see this in the way they hold their weight over the balls of the feet and seem to lean slightly forward when they stand. When they walk, there is a forward-falling quality to their gait. This is because they were more interested in getting somewhere than in establishing independent vertical support, so they probably just crawled up a wall or a chair to reach their feet and tumbled onward toward the object of their interest.

If you encounter people who carry their weight on the balls of the feet, you are approaching Forward Fallers. These individuals are always moving toward the next objective and bounding ahead. They are going to look at you, and if interested, make you part of their next experience. Let them present themselves; let them talk. You listen. Forward Fallers like to talk about their dreams so you can relate to them. They like to be heard, and in the process, they will form a picture of you.

They are always ready to leap into the next experience or the next new situation. Perhaps they seem impetuous to you. I can tell you that if they are emotionally close to you, then you must have chosen them for this quality. They developed the postural alignment they have today by always being anxious to see what the world had in store for them next. They are people who did not bother establishing independent vertical support in the process of learning to walk in the first place. They just got their head up high enough to see what interesting things lay before them and charged off to get in there.

They are people who usually felt safe exploring their world, or grew up with parents or guardians who were always there and would extract them from anything too serious into which the young Forward Fallers adventured.

My friend Anne is very much a Forward Faller. Truthful to the image of an inverted pyramid ready to fall in any direction, she is always ready to charge ahead with any idea that appeals to her. This makes her an exciting friend, if a slightly impulsive one. Strangely enough, she is also very shy. She needs to be approached softly, because she can also bolt away if she perceives danger from another person.

Dealing With Torso-Sway Walkers

Torso-Sway Walkers first established a wide base of vertical support as children because they felt challenged and vulnerable. This wider base of psychological support helped them maintain their place in the world and in relation to other people.

Torso-Sway Walkers are people who have a coherent understanding of their own reality. They fit you into it as part of their context. In other words, they are going to look at you from their place, and you will fit into it (or not), depending on the way you present yourself. Barging ahead and demanding of them to participate in your world is not likely to get a good response. On the other hand, allowing them to present themselves will allow you to fit yourself into their world. So sit back, be patient, and let them weave their world in front of you.

If an important person in your world stands with this naturally wide base of support, feet slightly turned out and about shoulder-width apart, he is probably a

Torso-Sway Walker. As a child, he felt that he had to struggle to be recognized, or he felt a little threatened by life. Maybe he lived in a crowded environment where he felt that he might be knocked down if he did not stand with a wide, powerful base. Maybe he was just naturally strong-willed and met with opposition in the form of other siblings. He might even have been the only child of very intelligent parents, and therefore felt the need to prove himself constantly.

For whatever reason, they are individuals that felt the need to prove something, or at least prove they could hold their own ground. They may even have a maddening tendency to tell everyone the same stories they once told you. This is just their way of affirming themselves to the world. Perhaps they fought long and hard to become who they are and just need to remind themselves, even though you never doubt them at all. This is a developmental pattern we see a lot with children who grow up in a marginalized neighborhood or in an abusive household. Anywhere a child feels threatened physically or emotionally can bring about this "ever-preparedness" to be knocked around physically or mentally. So give these individuals the opportunity to let you know where they are coming from. It is important to them that you understand who they are.

A man I once met at a business meeting was a Torso-Sway Walker. He stood with his feet shoulder-width apart, and he swayed from side to side as he walked. He was the vice president of a major telemarketing company and wanted to distribute a video about Bio-Typing. He announced his importance by being late for the meeting that had brought us several hundred miles to attend. He then proceeded, unnecessarily, to describe his company and his role in it. As the meeting went on, we began to realize that everything was going to be discussed on his terms and only on his terms.

Naturally, I saw this as the ideal opportunity to tell him about the Torso-Sway Walker Bio-Type. I should have followed my own advice and just kept on nodding until he was finished. With my shins sore from being kicked repeatedly by my wife, I soon sat back and listened, nodding frequently. When he ran low on batteries, I restated his own statement of purpose and dovetailed my project into it. He was impressed with my understanding of him and his company and wanted to do business with us.

Today, when I see a man or a woman standing with feet shoulder-width apart and chin with a slight forward thrust, I anticipate the naturally strong mental stance of a Torso-Sway Walker.

What about Yourself?

As one of these Bio-Types, learn to recognize that your own tendencies are just your own take on things—neither better nor worse, merely your own.

If you are a Backward Faller, you like to hear what another person has to say. You are by nature independent and self-reliant. As a child, you got to your feet without the use of any external support, and today you tend to stand by your opinions without the need of external confirmation. When you are faced with a new person in your world, you study that person; taking in everything you can detail-by-detail. Then and only then will you begin to open up to allow a more personal encounter.

If you are a Forward Faller, when you see someone who interests you, you may find yourself charging forward into a relationship with that person. You will be involved before you even have taken the time to know them. You are more immediate, more interested in the future of possibilities.

If you are a Torso-Sway Walker, you observe someone from the strength of your position and analyze how that person correlates with your world. Only if you feel that person fits somewhere into it, will you decide to let him in. If that person really fascinates you, you might shift your wide base of support and throw yourself into an entirely new alignment—a new juxtaposition—to take him in.

If You Are a Forward Faller

As a Forward Faller, you seem to see the end result of what you are doing more clearly than the individual steps you will have to take to get there.

With Backward Fallers, don't worry or react if they are not as excited as you, and they focus instead on the steps necessary to get the result. Remember that Backward Fallers see everything as a process and a series of steps. They are not implying you cannot reach your goal by immediately questioning you about each aspect. In fact, the very opposite is true. Your listener is interested enough to be looking seriously at how you will be able to achieve what it is you want to do.

With Torso-Sway Walkers, remember that they are like pyramids, firmly planted in their ideas. So do not try to move them. Instead, try to see yourself from their context, honor it, and then show how your point relates to what they already believe. This means that you are going to have to acknowledge where the Torso-

Sway Walker is coming from first. Show that you respect his point of view or position, and then figure out how to relate your communication to some idea or experience of his own. It is not that he is not interested; it is merely that he needs to find something personal to hook into in order to relate to it to himself and his own viewpoint.

If a friend stands firmly rooted over a wide base of support expecting opposition, remember that he or she might not have had the unconditional support that you always felt around you. Now is the opportunity to provide that same environment of unconditional love for them when they need it!

With another Forward Faller, know that they are like an avalanche that is about to rumble; so clear the ground ahead and give them an exciting nudge in the right direction. It will be perfectly fine to describe in detail the finished dream, leave out the rest, and trust that they will deal with obstacles as they arise.

If You Are a Backward Faller

As a Backward Faller, you might tend to get so caught up in the steps of the process that you might lose sight of the dream for a while.

When dealing with Forward Fallers, it will mean putting the steps involved on hold and focusing on the outcome, the dream, if you will. If you are a producer or an executive with others working for you, how you present tasks to your subordinates requires different descriptions of the tasks for different Bio-Types. If you want Forward Fallers to work well on a part of the project, give them a goal they can visualize and a way for them to know when they have achieved it. This may mean breaking the overall project down into stages and making the completion of each stage a separate goal.

If your friends who are Forward Fallers seem to live with their head buried in the clouds, you may not really need to point out all the obvious obstacles in their path before they run into the obstacles themselves. There will always be time to make your point when they become stuck, and it will be a good opportunity to show them all the things you are good at stockpiling in anticipation of future needs. Telling Forward Fallers what is obviously going to be a problem tomorrow today will seem like a lack of faith, even if it is really only loving support. They might surprise you at their innate ability to stay balanced, even as they overcome obstacles which might temporarily paralyze you.

With Torso-Sway Walkers, you are going to have to first acknowledge where they are coming from. Show that you respect their point of view or their position, and then figure out how to relate your communication to some idea or experience of their own. It is not that they are not interested; it is merely that they need to find something personal to hook into in order to relate to it to themselves and their own viewpoint. In designing a project, be sure that they see their place and their part in it.

With other Backward Fallers, define the overall goal of the project, and then let them familiarize themselves with their own portion of it. They will map their own path to complete it. They will be interested in the entire process and will want to see where they fit in and what their personal responsibility will be.

If You Are a Torso-Sway Walker

As a Torso-Sway Walker, you might be a little too concerned about the way things are and not open enough to the way someone else might see how they could be.

When dealing with a Forward Faller, you might have to resist the urge to ask, "What, exactly, does this have to do with me?" The "my way or the highway" attitude can sometimes get in the way of hearing a new idea or plan that might really appeal to you, if you can succeed in putting aside your own views.

With a Backward Faller, not only must you resist the urge to ask, "What, exactly, does this have to do with me?" You must also educate yourself in following the step-by-step presentation of an idea that seems totally outside of your own context.

With other Torso-Sway Walkers, you need to remember your own tendency toward inflexibility and learn to find ways to align yourself with their experiences and viewpoints. Then you can show them how your idea is not that different from their own.

Solving Conflicts

Common sense and humility apply. Do not ask other people to see, think and do things the way you do. Instead, learn to understand what you can about their communication style first.

In my own life, once I have established this, I can figure out how I would have to rephrase what I want to say in order to get them to respond the way I would like them to respond. Then I get to decide whether I am willing to do or say what is necessary. It helps me to pause to reflect on the way I naturally say and do things and decide if it is really the best way in this circumstance.

When you are able to distinguish the differences between yourself and others, you can enjoy the freedom in relating with other people. When you are able to distinguish the differences between yourself and others, you can use that knowledge to shift your view of the world to include theirs. Then you will be using the best means to approach them and communicate with them.

When You Meet Someone for the First Time

I once heard a re-known author speaking at a convention. I knew she was one of the first people I had ever met who truly saw the world from a place that was similar to where I lived. As soon as she finished her presentation, I simply had to make contact with her. I knew that she would be signing a few books and then returning to the other side of the country where she lived, and I would never be able to get to know her. I rushed up to the stage and got a few seconds to introduce myself before she was whisked away by her handlers. I said I really wanted to talk to her. She indicated that I could go to the table where the book signing was. I did.

When I got there, I told her I was working on a book and that it was about reading people by the way they walked. She turned her head at an angle and looked at me. I mentioned that by the way she walked, I knew that she was naturally a keen observer of people, that she was methodical in her ways of doing things, that she was probably a good teacher and that she probably tended to have tension in her neck.

People who wanted her to sign their books for them were mobbing her and she could not exactly take the time to converse with me. However, she was fascinated that I was aware of so much about her before I had even met her. She gave me the email address for her publisher, said I must use a password that would let her know it was I, and told me she would write back. Today she is one of my closest friends.

When Dealing With Other Bio-Types

With Forward Fallers; be sure to be goal-oriented, looking toward results for requested efforts.
Tell them what they are going to get out of the situation.

With Backward Fallers, be sure to be methodical and process-oriented.
Be specific about the steps taken thus far and those to take in the future.

With Torso-Sway Walkers, be sure to be interested in their background.
Relate what you have to say to what they have told you about themselves.

9

Bio-Typing in the Business World

Once Upon a Time in Japan

It is a cold early morning. You are standing at the edge of a clearing. There is an icy, cutting wind blowing all around you. The first yellow rays of the morning sun silhouette the head and the shoulders of a man standing very still. He is about ten feet away, facing you, his entire concentration focused on every one of your movements. The hilt of a killing sword is jutting out from his hip. It is a "katana," a four-foot piece of steel capable of easily cutting a man in half.

The swordsman wearing it is a Samurai warrior, unafraid of death. Through a lifetime of training, he has learned to use his weapon with breathtaking speed and precision. Imagine, now, that you also are a Samurai warrior. Neither of you has any doubts about the issue of this encounter; it will be mortal combat. To stay alive, you must predict with absolute accuracy when and how your opponent will attack. To win, you have to identify, at a glance, the weak spots in his defense and exploit them. A failure to do so will find you dead or dismembered before you even know you have lost.

What would it be like if you could begin your next important presentation with inside information about the associates you are facing? What if you knew how to phrase your presentation before you even opened your mouth; so that you were able to capture your associates' attention and their imagination? What if you could anticipate their weaknesses, know the ways to throw them off their concentration or sidetrack them when you wanted to?

What if you could know how best to present your ideas and make your requests before you the walk into your boss's office?

What if "cold calls" were suddenly not so cold because you had a clear idea, even over the phone, of the other person's Bio-Type within the first few responses he makes to your greeting?

Eight-hundred years ago in feudal Japan, legendary samurai swordsmen were able to size up their opponents so thoroughly by observing them stand and walk that the samurais knew exactly how to engage a fight and what to watch out for. The average length of combat took a handful of seconds, after which, the opponent less prepared lay either dead on the ground or wishing he'd been killed rather than be so severely mutilated. To win meant being the best at clearly predicting the other fighter's "flow of energy" or "Ki," knowing which movements would naturally flow better for him; and which ones would not. Life or death proved right from wrong.

These people had already found out that the way we do things with our bodies reflects precisely the way we do things with our minds. If, for instance, we hold our weight forward over the balls of our feet, ready to leap into action, so do we also hold our mental focus ready to commit to tackle new problems quickly, ready to strike at the first occasion. If we hold our weight back over our heels, we are more likely to take a moment to assess a problem and its possible solutions before we jump in, cleverly planning to avoid the first blow, finding a weak spot in the other's defense and rendering death in the counter-strike.

Modern businesspeople are not all that different from ancient samurai warriors. They size each other up, looking for openings. They measure their associates, looking for weaknesses in their presentations or organizations. Business negotiations may have replaced sword fights, but the eagerness to win is still the same.

Just as the sword fighters used feints and thrusts to probe for openings, so must successful 21st century negotiators learn to test, observe and assess as accurately as possible when others are bluffing and when they are strong. What do they listen for in a presentation? How do they solve problems? Who is likely to make a quick decision based upon their instincts? Who will be naturally inclined to assemble and analyze all the data they can get before choosing the most advantageous course of action? Who is most concerned about where you are coming from?

All of these answers are written clearly in the way businesspeople hold their bodies and in how they phrase their questions. They are listening to hear things presented in a way they can relate to, a way that feels familiar. They are looking for good answers from you.

Business methods in Japan show how much people there never lost the sacred knowledge inherited from their ancestors, the samurai. When Western businesspersons travel to Japan, they are often surprised to find that many hours (if not days!) of polite and apparently inane conversation always precede any real business negotiations. Their hosts discuss the weather, health in the families of the participants and other seemingly trivial matters before they eventually get down to business. Unfortunately, all too often, inexperienced Westerners are bored and fidget their way through this Eastern adversary-assessment period.

Asian people have long known that an adversary "gives away the store" while discussing his garden and hobbies. That inordinately long "waste of time" preceding negotiations is anything but a waste of time. The Asians reading their adversary, and they are careful to say little about their own true feelings, lest they allow themselves to be read. This is why they tend to sit very still at the negotiating table. They are all too aware of just how much about their minds is revealed in even the smallest movements of their bodies.

If only you could get the opposition to answer those 60 to 300 specific questions from the Myers-Briggs Type Indicator or get their astrological sun sign and rising sign. Needless to say, this is not very likely in business negotiations. Hiding true feelings is an art among professionals in business. However, you cannot avoid walking, breathing and standing. Observing is all a person familiar with Bio-Typing knowledge requires to determine everything he needs to be successful in business.

Having Bio-Typed yourself, you have already begun seeing the differences from one person to the next. Now we take the art of diagnosing another person's Bio-Type out in the field and begin to apply it.

Let's Get Down to Business

How successfully your message gets across to someone, such as a customer, depends a lot on how you present it. You do not want to rub someone the wrong way, so it is important that you present what you have to say in a way in which he is naturally prepared to listen. Each of the three Bio-Types listens in a different way. Each needs specific things from you in order to key in to what you are presenting. Each has turn-offs you must avoid.

(1)   *(2)*   *(3)*

Figure 43: (1) Torso-Sway Walker, (2) Backward Faller, (3) Forward Faller.

When you are at a meeting of several people and you can take just a few seconds to determine the Bio-Types of everyone there before you begin, things may flow dramatically differently than if you do not. Knowing individual Bio-Types allows you to make the best possible opening approach to each of the participants, and you will be also able to choose which information to present to which individual.

The "dream" or end result of your pitch needs to be aimed at the individuals most focused on it, the Forward Fallers, if there any present. The "steps to getting there" will be the primary concern of the Backward Fallers. The "Where you are coming from?" portion should be aimed at the Torso-Sway Walkers.

Torso-Sway Walkers (figure 43, #1) stand with their feet separated to about shoulder-width and turned outward. They walk with a side-to-side, torso-shifting gait. When they inhale, they spread their ribcages to the sides. They bend from the hips when they bend down to pick something up, keeping their back more straight or plank-like.

Backward Fallers (figure 43, #2) stand with their feet about two inches apart, either parallel or slightly turned outward. Their heads shift slightly from-side-to-side when they walk. When they inhale, they arch their backs. They also bend from the hips when they bend down to pick something up.

Forward Fallers (figure 43, #3) tend to have their heels together. When they walk, their heads remain centered, not moving side-to-side at all. They do not arch their back when they inhale. When they bend down, it is from the waist, creating the appearance of a more rounded back.

It is not complicated to know what to do with this information about Bio-Types. Forward Fallers will respond to hearing the dream in all its glory. Backward Fallers will respond to all the carefully detailed steps you plan to take in achieving that dream. Torso-Sway Walkers will listen once they are convinced that where you are coming from is similar to where they are coming from.

In business, it is sometimes necessary to keep your adversary off-guard for various reasons, such as to get more information from him than he might normally want to share or to keep him from seeing some weaker aspects of your hoped-for deal.

You must also be aware of your own tendencies when you communicate! Being aware of what you are inclined to do will help you to know what you should systematically watch for when you talk.

If You Are a Forward Faller

If you are a Forward Faller, you are quick at seeing opportunities and knowing where you would like to arrive. Learn to stop and plan things logically and in sequence before presenting anything important to Backward Fallers. Rather than focusing on what the fulfilled idea will be like, think through the steps that will get you there. Torso-Sway Walkers are put off by people whose heads are in the fulfillment of their own dream, so present your idea in the context of the Torso-Sway Walkers' beliefs and goals. Be wary of rushing things and saying more than you intend.

If You Are a Backward Faller

If you are a Backward Faller, your tendency is to present things in a linear fashion, going from point to point. You naturally present things in a descriptive and analytical manner, and will naturally bore Forward Fallers, who do not concern themselves much with the details of your plans They want to hear about the big picture and its benefits, so get there quickly. As for Torso-Sway Walkers, they do not like to hear intellectual, step-by-step descriptions of any given project, either. Help them to find something personal, something that is directly related to their experiences or their beliefs in what you are talking about. Find something that they can hook into so they can relate it to their own experience. You probably also wait for someone to 'break the ice' before you begin, being naturally reticent to speak first.

If You Are a Torso-Sway Walker

If you are a Torso-Sway Walker, you may tend to fall into long monologues. Refrain from describing your theories on the subject at hand in great length. Stay factual, and educate yourself in following the step-by-step presentation of an idea favored by Backward Fallers when you talk to them. Describe the "big picture" and its benefits to Forward Fallers. Be aware that you repeat what you have already said several times, so cut it short. For you, less is more. The less you talk, the more they will listen.

If The Person You Are Speaking to Is a Forward Faller

In business, Forward Fallers hold their weight over the balls of their feet, always ready to move into action. They are goal-oriented and want to hear about the "big picture" and its benefits, not what steps are necessary to get there. Let them first describe their plans and dreams to you. Acknowledge what they have accomplished, and then lead them toward the new dream that you are creating. Talk to them about what the future is going to look like when they do what you are suggesting. Get them excited, and they will follow you. Do not get yourself (and them!) bogged down in overstating the steps along the way in order to ascertain they have really thought their idea through and aren't skipping over things that will trip you both up. They solve dilemmas in motion and do not need to think it all through before choosing to act.

If the Person You Are Speaking to Is a Backward Faller

Backward Fallers hold their weight on their heels. They first want to hear what you have to say before they say what they think. Remember, they were independent children who got to their feet independently of external support. They got first one foot and then the other under themselves and then used their back muscles to lift their heads as high as possible to see what was around them. Backward Fallers always observe before they move forward. They plan things out logically and in sequence before taking any action or accepting any new individual. Be aware that they are better at listening and responding or at modifying your proposals than at taking the lead.

Do you remember my wife? She moves along a track of her own style. If I want to tell her something, I need to get her attention and then proceed logically, within a context that is familiar to her. While Forward Fallers may be ready to leap into something new and exciting on a whim, Backward Fallers need to feel that what you are proposing makes sense before they will climb aboard. Once on board, the Backward Faller will design his own map and follow it to the end.

If the Person You Are Talking to Is a Torso-Sway Walker

Torso-Sway Walkers like to maintain a strong physical foundation, with feet spread widely when they stand and their body weight well distributed over each foot. They hold an equally strong foundation in their beliefs and self-image and need to understand at all times where things and people fit into their world and how they relate to it. It is best to let them speak first. You listen.

They believe that you, like them, need to understand who they are, where they are coming from and what the relationship between the two of you is. Sit back, be patient and let them lay out a picture of their world in front of you. They will be truly ready to hear about your ideas afterwards—not before. When your time comes, establish a context with them. Acknowledge where they are coming from and honor it. Then show them how your viewpoint relates to some idea or experience of their own or to what they already believe. They need to find something personal in what you are talking about to hook into so they can relate to it.

Do you remember my friend Veronica? She always stands planted firmly, with her feet separated and slightly turned outward. Can you remember her sitting for hours at the dinner table resolutely refusing to eat her vegetables? I told you how she, like all Torso-Sway Walkers, needed to establish who she was against a world that felt threatening to her. Remember how she established a strong, wide base of support so as not to be knocked over? Well, now just imagine her in a business suit.

What If You Cannot See the Person You Are About to Do Business With?

What if you are talking to a stranger you have never seen? Business is often done over the phone. What value, then, does Bio-Typing have?

Learning to listen to the way people talk is a lot like looking at how they stand and walk. Remember that Bio-Typing a person is all about watching the way that different individuals accomplish similar actions in different ways. What about assessing someone speaking to you on the phone or assessing the questions they might ask you about what you are presenting. Every conversation is full of certain standard, common verbal interactions.

You: "Hello, my name is."
The other person: "Where did you get my name?"
You: "Yes, I got your name and number from so-and-so."
The other person: "What are you offering me, exactly?"
And so on.

Learning to discern the different methods different individuals use for these common interactions can lead to the discovery of the person's Bio-Type, and discovering a person's Bio-Type is the key to successful interactions in person or on the phone.

Remember that Backward Fallers are observing before making a decision to engage with you. Therefore, they will ask several questions about who you are, why you are calling them, where you got their number from in the first place. If your answers do not make clear sense, they will disconnect from you before you ever get to make your pitch. If their initial questions and responses follow this pattern, approach them slowly and in a step-by-step and informative manner.

Remember that Forward Fallers are impetuous and into adventure. If the voice on the other end of the phone responds to your initial opening with a question about what you are offering, do not lay a foundation about who you are or where you are calling from. Offer them a dream, and let them ask you about the details.

If you are speaking to Forward Fallers, they will want to know what is in it for them.

If the voice answering the phone is that of a Torso-Sway Walker, his first questions to you will be about why he should stop what he is doing to discuss anything with you. Lay down the foundation that will make him feel you share common interests and common goals. It will take some work to get there Torso-Sway Walker interested and willing to commit, but be ready to close the deal when "critical mass" is achieved.

Try to grasp a firm picture of the people you are doing business with as the children they were, instead of as the shielded personalities hidden behind the expensive suits and facades they present. The idea is not to manipulate them, but rather to understand them and relate to them from a place where they can be comfortable and geared toward mutually beneficial goals. I never advocate manipulation of others, and I believe mutual benefit will always be more profitable. However, if you must think in terms of gaining advantage, think of the "samurai concept" of getting the adversary to tell more about himself than he might intend.

Knowing how various individuals see themselves in relation to their world can give you a lot of important information for getting the best out of them as co-workers or associates.

Getting the Best out of Your Co-workers

Just as home life can flow more smoothly if you and your close ones take Bio-Type differences into consideration; this is also true of the workplace. Knowing the strengths and weaknesses of each individual in a group can always make that group's efforts better. Ignoring differences in the ways people you work with take in information, approach tasks and interface with each other can never make for good feelings and the best joint efforts.

Give Goal-Oriented Assignments to Forward Fallers

I once read a book about a Roman gladiator. He was a great fighter, because he always seemed to know in advance when his opponent was going to attack and when he was merely bluffing. This gladiator would amuse the crowds by not taking any defensive action until the precise moment when a real attack was launched. He explained that by watching the feet of his opponent, he would see the digging in of the back heel before a real spear-throw and not be deceived by the movements of the upper body.

If you look at my friend James' feet, you see that he always has his weight shifted forward over the balls of his feet. This tells me he is always ready to leap forward into action. Remember, Backward Fallers carry their weight back over the heels and thus have to shift it forward over the balls of their feet before launching forward. This is not so for the Forward Fallers of this world.

With a client and friend named Ann, I learned quickly to keep the nature of Forward Fallers in mind before I opened my mouth. I was trying to demonstrate something about lines of force; and how we can use them to intercept the forces coming toward us. I stupidly said, "Imagine you are a throwing fist toward my face."

Well, she hit me! She took my words, saw what I was asking and gave it to me. Where the Backward Faller would have considered and weighed the possibilities involved, the Forward Faller is more likely to envision things as a fait accompli and jump in!

Forward Fallers can bring enthusiasm and great visions of what could be. Remember that they can provide motivation when you might be a little uncertain of what exactly you want. Unfettered by too much reality-based detail, they bring great dreams and visions of what could be, and they naturally have the energy to surmount difficult details as they arise. In a team, they are the people who supply the energy to fuel the realization of a project. Forward Fallers are the individuals who leap into the new and the unknown, leaving behind everything to pursue the goal, which is their primary concern. They will commit to tackling new problems quickly and be eager for new experiences and sensations.

Forward Fallers are powerful allies, as long as you can keep them focused on the important dream—yours. Do note that at some point, they might also start to see your dream as their own. Make sure, then, that they do not start dreaming a different dream from yours! If you want them to work well, give them a goal they can visualize, and tell them what it will look like so that they can know when they have achieved it. This may mean breaking down the overall project into stages and making the completion of each stage a separate goal.

Always remember that people who insist upon taking a step-by-step approach naturally irritate Forward Fallers. So stay in the background if your tendency is to consider all of the ramifications of a plan before you act. The way of Forward Fallers is to handle problems, as they arise, not before. If you are the manager, oversee their activity in a general sense, and make yourself available to help them work out all of the possible pitfalls along their path. Forward Fallers are so good at seeing the final result that they often do not look carefully at the terrain ahead and might slam into obstacles that Backward Fallers, for example, would have foreseen and planned for in advance.

Allow Backward Fallers to Do What They Do Best Naturally

When my wife is on the computer, I know to let her explore what happens if she does this or that. When she wants to know how to do something specific, and has exhausted all her ideas, then she is ready to hear how I might do it. She loves to see what each and every command does and will spend hours trying things that seem to be a diversion from what I think she should be focusing on, finishing up so she can be with me! She needs to try things in her own fashion first, and her learning curve is fantastic once she has completed her initial testing and exploring.

Backward Fallers are organized and methodical. They bring great organizational and production skills to the job. Learn to use their natural strengths to get the job done. They are good at doing it, so let them run with the details! Their approach to life is linear, one thing at a time, and they see everything as a series of steps to take.

They can help you step back a little and plan the process that will best serve your ambitions, but be aware of their weakness. While Backward Fallers may think out a process in its entirety before doing anything, they may also have a tendency to lose sight of the overall goal they are trying to achieve; becoming buried in the steps along the way. As a manager, you can help them by reviewing their list of priorities on a regular basis to make sure they stay focused on the overall goal.

Do not micromanage them! Give them an assignment or a goal, and let them proceed, even if you see obstacles that they are about to hit. Do not intercede until they reach an impasse and are ready to hear your guidance. Then your advice will be welcome. If you offer your advice too soon, it will irritate them or make them feel that you lack faith in them, and add it to the list they are compiling against you.

Let Torso-Sway Walkers Provide the Stability and Cohesiveness That Comes Naturally to Them

Remember my friend Veronica. Standing as she naturally does with widely spread turned-out feet, she is not likely to be knocked over easily. Can you remember how she had to fight as a child to assert herself? Today, she still guards her position vigorously and needs to be certain you are taking her position seriously. Veronica may need to express her position to you one more time so she is sure you know where she is coming from before she will go where you want to direct her.

I once wanted to teach her an exercise series that could keep her from hurting her lower back. She is a serious bodybuilder with a terrific body, but she had to cut back on her weight training because of stress to her lower back. I knew a core-strengthening regime that would really make her happy and enable her to continue building her muscles safely. However, Veronica is a Torso-Sway Walker and is set in her ways of doing things.

If I had just started telling her what she should be doing, she would have dug in her heels and defended her current regime, even with the injuries she had sustained. It was not that she didn't trust me. On the contrary, it is rather that she had spent a lifetime defending her ways of doing things against outside interference.

In order to get her to open up to the possibility for a change, I knew I would have to first listen to how she already worked out, appreciating all the positive aspects of her routine. I had to let her assert her position, and then validate it. After that, I could begin to plant the idea of a specific situation where having added core stability would fit in perfectly with her training goals. She would then be ready to hear my thoughts. Otherwise, she would have politely let me run on, and she would have continued with her current regime.

Once I had validated her way of working out in a way that didn't threaten her, I called up for her the precise actions that had caused the pain in her lower back, and then suggested that she try doing the new set of actions. Once she tried it, she was willing to agree with me. If I had tried to override her mindset, I would have just pushed her away—maybe even caused her to be more firmly rooted in what she was doing.

Torso-Sway Walkers bring stability and constancy. They can be the hard-core person in the team, the one standing by the beliefs and traditions of the past. They can help you to see clearly why you are drawn toward a specific goal, whether that goal is right for you and how well it meshes with the larger picture. They are great individuals to choose if you want someone with solidity of character and nerves of strength or someone who can take a strong stand at the negotiating table. They will solidly hold to whatever position they have and still have the opportunity to swing 180 degrees if the need arises. Think of Bill Clinton. He is a typical Torso-Sway Walker.

10

A New Perspective in Parent/ Child Relationships

The human body, unfortunately, does not come with instructions.

Figure 44: My friend Sindi, a Backward Faller (notice the tilted back head) and the youngest of her three children, Astrid, a Forward Faller.

As I have mentioned, the origin of a person's Bio-Type is all in the choices he makes as a child in the uses of his muscles. I believe you can trace the muscle recruitment patterns of an adult back to those choices he made as a child. Why does one child make different choices than another child? What are the reasons for one choice versus another?

I believe each of us, as little children, already had the seeds of our developing personality even before we began to discover and use our bodies. Every child develops a sense of self. Part of this comes from his innate nature, that indefinable part of a person that seems to have been written into his DNA. Much of it comes from the way that his parents nurture him. Some parents allow the child to discover much of his world all by himself. Other parents want to be part of the discovery process. Some parents never let the child hit the floor when he falls. Other parents let the child discover the ups and downs of gravity without too much interference.

As a psychologist, my wife facilitates a parenting class. She tells me that in the earliest stages of a child's development, a child needs to be both protected and allowed to venture out and make discoveries, then to return to the protection of the parents. Too much protecting, and the child never learns to be responsible for taking risks, because the parent is always there to pick up the pieces. Too little protection and the child does not want to venture out for fear of getting into something he cannot handle. A child learns by receiving messages from his environment and from the modeling provided by caretakers. The child's first 18 months are significantly impacted by nurture, encouragement, exercise, nourishment and self-feeding, picking up and dropping things and making the messes that all children do! Parenting is not a skill that comes automatically or that we even have time to learn. Parents bumble though the initiation process drawing on whatever experiences they can!

When we first began to engage with our world, we did so with our bodies. If the body we live in today is the written history of our ways of doing things for a lifetime, then this history had to have begun somewhere. If you are a parent, you are watching history being written. Not only that, with a deeper awareness of the Bio-Type of your child, you can have a greater hand in shaping your child's life!

How Can This Be So?

We are now going to take look at how to see and appreciate the world as your child sees and experiences it. And, if I may, I would like to offer you some ideas on interacting in the most powerful way with the emerging personality of your child and make a few suggestions on assisting in the development both all the muscles of his body and his ability to use both sides of his brain. Then I will address designing actions and games to develop different muscle groups and problem-solving approaches your child might otherwise miss.

Sound exciting? Remember who I am and where I am coming from. As a child with autism, I most likely would have been condemned to a life of total disconnection from my world if my own mother had not actively intervened in my development. My friend Liane Holliday Willey says that people with high-functioning autism are the highest-ability members of a society of people with special gifts and special problems. Each of us that has reached this higher level of functionality has done so only because someone was able to see our world through our eyes, appreciate our viewpoint, and reach in to help us to better enter the world others naturally share. For Liane, that someone was her father. For me, it was my mother.

When I was a child, I spent my days banging my head into the back of chairs and my nights making holes in the wall at the head of my bed. I did this to help myself deal with all of the stimuli pouring into me because this input was coming in too fast for me to process. Repetitive, self-stimulating actions such as head banging perhaps also helped me in processing the day's experiences. I do not really know. All I know is that it felt better than lying still under the assault of impressions, sounds and feelings that were a like a tidal wave hitting my consciousness. Today I am a fully functioning adult who still rocks himself to sleep every night.

If your child is neurotypical, you are not facing the challenges my mother faced, but you can still learn to better appreciate and enter into the world of your child by taking in a few ideas of interpersonal-relations techniques from Bio-Typing.

When my mother found her precious Johnny dropping the family's eggs onto the kitchen floor, she found the patience to drop a few with me to discover the world of beauty in the transformation from white orb to multicolored hurricane on the linoleum. When she found me experimenting with the creation of bright red colors in fascinating flow patterns while I played with razor blades, she found the fortitude to also see things from my perspective not just her own.

What would it be like if you could bring your viewpoint onto the same level as that of your child? What if you could watch and participate as he developed his personality? What would it be like if you could form a deeper appreciation of the differences between your ways of seeing things and your child's?

Until now, we have been going backwards to try to discover the child we once were. Now let us look at the child who is just creating himself and maybe assist in that development through conscious interaction across Bio-Type differences.

Let Us Begin By Bio-Typing Your Child

Bio-Typing children require a few practical considerations. For one, the hips of an infant are splayed out to the sides for the first months of crawling. Until the hips are drawn together, there can be no certainty about possible Bio-Types.

You just have to wait patiently until your child begins to crawl with his legs together and begin to reach for a standing position on his own. Be wary of helping the child to walk and to climb to his feet in an assisted manner. Doing so can jump-start certain muscles and discourage the discovery of others. It would more advantageous to intervene once the child has gotten to his feet in his own natural progression of getting there. I personally also distrust manufactured baby-walker equipment because it, too, sabotages the natural discovery and development of the postural and walking muscles.

Let us zoom ahead to the time when your child begins to crawl cohesively, which happens once his belly is off the floor. By this point, he is reaching out toward something. The desire to stand up and then to begin walking has come. Prior to this stage, all his efforts have been to making his arms and legs respond to his muscles.

Determining Your Child's Bio-Type

What do you, as a parent, really see when you look at your child? What can you learn about how your child sees his world just by closely observing the way his body moves through it?

Just as you have learned to observe adults doing the same actions differently, let us now begin to see our children. While you may get hints as to your child's Bio-Type along the way, it is very important to remember to wait until the child has actually begun to climb to his feet in an attempt to start walking before you seek to Bio-Type him with any clarity.

We are going to see what new facts you can learn about your child's world by applying some of the principles of Bio-Typing to the observation of children. We will start by looking at how your child is presently using his body.

Personality is strongly defined by how we go about seeing things, approaching things, doing things and responding to things. Can you think of any description of personality that is not about how a person approaches, sees, does or responds to life?

The most primary actions of the infant, those used to crawl and to stand up over the feet, are self-defining. I believe these actions are also self-determining. By nature, some children are more impulsive, and others are less so. Some are more observant, some less so. Some children give little or no thought to the possibility of falling or of getting hurt and others are more cautious. More importantly, the child's physical activity is consequential because an active body sends messages to the brain that stimulate synaptic growth.

How a child sees himself in relation to his world is significant. It can be the result of how closely the parent watches over him, or it can be the result of the child taking a bad tumble at some point and getting frightened by the incident. Yet even given two children taking identical tumbles, each might respond differently to the experience. One might forget it as soon as it is over, and the other may live in fear of it happening again. You can sometimes help the child who falls to put a tumble into perspective by your reaction to the fall. There is the old story of a child terrified by an encounter with a snake. One parent tells the child to forget it, it did not happen. Another parent asks the child to tell her all about what the snake looked like, where it was etc. which child will harbor a life long fear of snakes?

The Art of Crawling

Like most actions, crawling can be done in a few different ways. Until now, we have been observing differences in breathing, walking and balancing; now let us consider possibilities with respect to crawling.

Some children crawl in a unilateral pattern. This is where the right hand and the right knee move forward, and then the left hand and knee come forward. There is also the pattern where the right hand and the left knee move forward, followed by the left hand and knee. What is the difference?

Science has discovered that the muscles actions on one side of the body are controlled by the opposite side of the brain. In other words, the left hand is controlled by the right side of the brain, and the left side of the brain controls the right hand.

The interface between the two hemispheres can be more or less fluid for different individuals. Just ask several of your friends to bring their left knees up to touch their right hands and their right knees up to their left hands in rapid succession and you will notice great variations in fluidity. Some people can do this alternation quickly and easily, others get confused and falter, and others are stuck.

The crawl test looks at the left/right (cross-lateral) or right/right (unilateral) actions of the arms and legs. It thus tests the rapidity of the interface between the left and right hemispheres of the brain. I believe this fluidity comes from the moving of alternate sides of the body as early as a child's crawling phase. If the cross-lateral interface is fluid, the child naturally crawls in a cross-lateral manner. If the cross-lateral interface is not fluid, the child naturally crawls in a unilateral manner.

The reason this is important is that different things take place in each of the two hemispheres. The right hemisphere is generally considered to be the seat of intuition and emotion. The left hemisphere is considered to be the place of logic and analysis. The facility of the interface between the two halves of the brain can have a lot to do with how easily a child can go from logical thought to intuitive thought. Developing increased crossover between the two sides of the body can dramatically increase the child's ability to go from logical thinking to intuitive thinking.

You may not be able to change your child's natural way of crawling, but being aware of the fluidity between the two sides of the brain can alert you to the idea of playing games with your child that involve the simultaneous use of the right hand and the left leg.

Can you think of games you could create to stimulate your child to move the left hand and right foot at the same time? Doing so early on might assist your child in developing the ability to think and act simultaneously and thus increasing his ability to shift from analytical thinking to intuitive thinking.

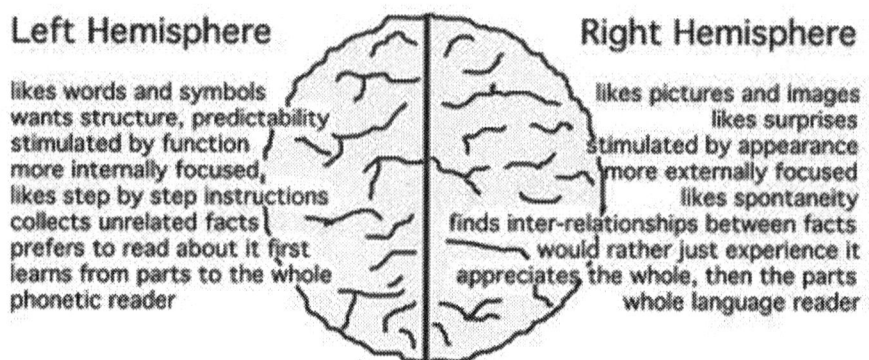

Left Hemisphere

likes words and symbols
wants structure, predictability
stimulated by function
more internally focused,
likes step by step instructions
collects unrelated facts
prefers to read about it first
learns from parts to the whole
phonetic reader

Right Hemisphere

likes pictures and images
likes surprises
stimulated by appearance
more externally focused
likes spontaneity
finds inter-relationships between facts
would rather just experience it
appreciates the whole, then the parts
whole language reader

Figure 45: Left and right brain hemispheres.

"There is a tendency for the two cerebral hemispheres to operate in two very different contexts: with most people (right-handed) the left is verbal/logical and the right side is non-verbal/intuitive, another words, left hemisphere is for verbal and analytical thought, the right for intuitive, philosophical, holistic patterns of thinking: primarily verbal mathematical and numerical concerned with paradox and pattern prefers holistic concepts.

"What they name left brain's linear knowledge and right brain's holistic knowing are not necessarily alternative, they can be mutually enriching. Making the hemispheres working together, even on very simple tasks including the movements, helps to promote their interactions.

"An important bundle of nerve fibers called the "corpus callosum" is situated between the right and left hemispheres. The left and right sides of the brain communicate with each other via this neural pathway. It is thought that "crossing" movements, when the right and left sides of the body work reciprocally, force hemispheres to co-operate. The pattern "right arm-left leg, then left arm-right leg" is used, for example, in walking."

Brain Hemispheres
By Dr. Tanya Zilberter
Web DietAndBody.com http://www.dietandbody.com/article1164.html

Which Bio-Type Best Describes Your Child?

Forward Faller Children

These precocious children are impatient to get started on the path of life. They may be charging forward already. You will observe these youngsters heading toward things ambitiously from the get-go. They are children who use objects along the way merely as tools to reach the all-important standing position. This standing position, however, is not the goal.

This child will naturally stand with the weight of the body forward over the balls of the feet. As a consequence, when they fall, they will tend to fall face first.

Forward Faller children do not stop there to make an independent stand. They leave that for the Backward Faller children. Verticality is just a station for Forward Faller children to pass through on their way forward. They have a serious goal in mind; to get a closer look at whatever it was that caught their attention in the first place. Whatever it takes to get there is irrelevant. They will always be falling forward toward the next discovery. Forward Faller children will not be interested in independent verticality! Once over the feet, they will not stop to establish independent vertical support before falling forward into the next step.

Figure 46: The Forward Faller Child climbs up an object in a quest for verticality.

Watch for the handy wall or chair on the way, which he uses to help him climb to his feet. The act of getting to his feet in the first place is just a problem to solve on his way. A Forward Faller is not concerned about what he is, but about where he is going.

Later in childhood, Forward Faller children will be able to shift quickly from emotional to analytical. They will also make important decisions based upon their feelings as often as upon logic, letting one inform the other.

As a young person, he will continue to barrel forward throughout his life. Look forward to his becoming an inventor, an adventurer, maybe even a leader. He will not wait for others to catch up before he charges into the next new thing. He will probably choose a profession where he is always doing new and exciting things. You may hear him ask, "Mom, why are these people all following me all the time?" People will follow him because a Forward Faller child knows where he wants to go and what he wants to see.

Forward Faller children may also be quite comfortable dealing with several people at the same time.

Watch to see how your Forward Faller child begins his career as an adult in the quest of something that totally captured his attention.

What Is the Best Way to Relate With Your Forward Faller Child?

Because these children are always diving forward into new situations and experiences, Forward Fallers need to learn to stop to observe the things taking place around them. They need to be taught to remain in one place long enough to catalogue all of the information around them before diving in, because they are always leaping forward into new situations and experiences. As a parent, you have built a strong sense of security around them, so they understand you will always be there for them. Now, seek to play games that show them how to foresee and avoid obstacles with a bit of advance planning. Play games of observation and testing of what is there to be seen.

The Backward Faller Children

These observant children will be preoccupied with each step of the process. They will get the idea that if both feet were under them, they might be able to raise their head higher to get a better look around them! Thus, the objective will be to get first one foot and then the other foot under themselves. Once this is accomplished, they will begin pushing with their legs against the floor until they reach an upright position. This process may be complicated, and will likely lead to more than one tumble backwards onto their bottom before victory is achieved. When they do get up onto their feet, they will do so entirely independently of any external support.

This child will naturally stand with the weight of the body back over the heels. When they do fall, they will tend to fall backwards onto their bottoms.

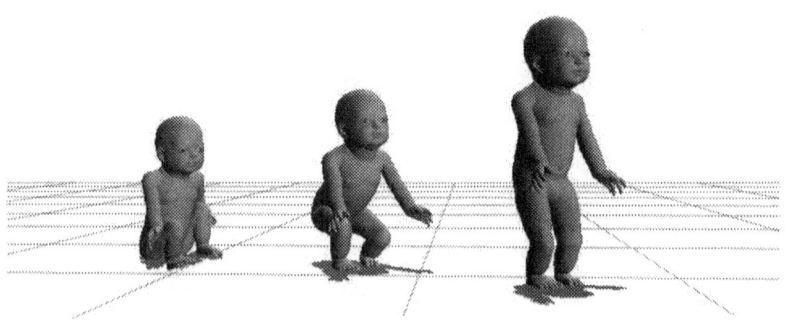

Figure 47: The Backward Faller Child gets to his feet independently of external support.

Backward Faller children are highly observant. Where Forward Faller children are all about getting somewhere, Backward Faller children prefer to look attentively at all the surroundings and absorb all the details before engaging in a response, and there is so much to look at!

This perhaps has a lot to do with why they will probably choose a profession where they will illuminate things for others. They will always be a good natural observer and will like to share their observations with others. With a Backward Faller child, look forward to a person who will show others what they may have overlooked. A journalist, a photographer, a teacher, producer or some other professional, he will guide others to see things that he naturally takes in. He will also be a good organizer. People will look at these individuals for appreciation and understanding of their world.

They will always be extremely independent and self-reliant. They will do every-thing in an orderly, step-by-step fashion: looking first, deciding where they want to proceed, and then moving forward, always absorbed in their process of getting there one step at a time.

These children like to do things in an experimental nature on their own. When someone else tells them how to do something "correctly," they will still want to do it their own way first just to try.

As they grow up, they are good at prioritizing things in their life and always pro-ceed in an orderly, systematic fashion. They would rather deal with things one at a time and in sequence than all at once.

What Is the Best Way to Relate With Your Backward Faller Child?

If your child is a Backward Faller, you might want to encourage him to try new things, take chances and leap. Hold out your arms, and teach him or her to fall into them.

They will want to stop to consider things and actions first, instead of letting their body just figure out how to do things by itself. Encourage Backward Faller chil-dren to move forward, not thinking so much how to get there.

These children can be so caught up in the steps of the process that they tend to lose sight of the overall goal they are trying to achieve. Playing games where they have to stay focused on what they are doing without losing sight of their goal will help them a lot.

They tend to be independent and strong-willed. They do not like to be given advice they did not ask for and much prefer to try things their own way first. Teach them to keep an open mind! They are thoughtful and observant but may sometimes seem slow and overly cautious. They want to do something 'right' on the first attempt, rather than to practice and learn from mistakes. Encourage them to try new things, take chances and leap into the unknown in order to develop trust in life. They need to learn to let their body do things naturally and trust in the outcome, rather than let their minds dissect every step and allow doubt, fear or uncertainty to paralyze their actions. Trying another approach is going to be uncomfortable for them, so honor their feelings of insecurity, and gradually convince them that they will be safe if they do what you want them to do (and make sure they really are safe).

The Torso-Sway Walker Children

These children will probably crawl for a longer time than other children will. Because they tend to feel challenged and vulnerable, they are more guarded in the process of getting to their feet.

Maybe they have a lot of brothers and sisters, or maybe they feel they are under a burden of expectation from those around them. They may also live in a world that is filled with things they feel threatened by, such as a loud neighborhood or a loud, crowded family environment. For whatever reason, they feel they need to establish their own autonomy in a definitive way. Their personality is forged in this same fire of resistance to being overwhelmed by their surroundings.

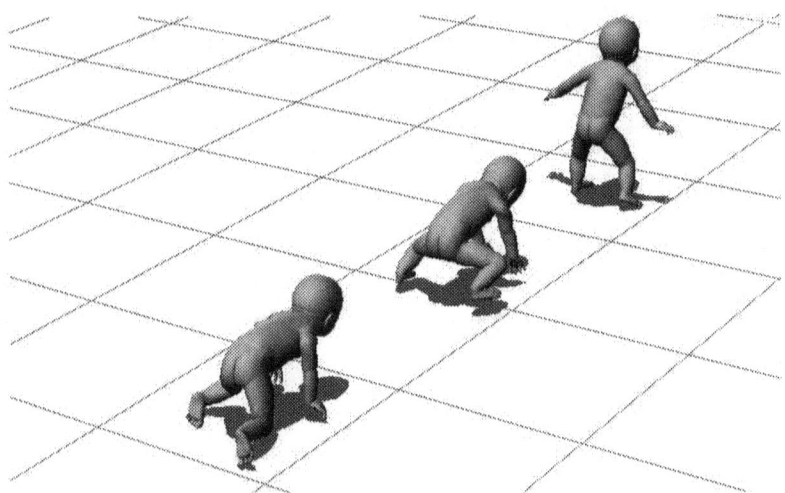

Figure 48: A Torso-Sway Walker child uses both hands and both feet to reach verticality.

These children will crawl on their hands and knees for a longer period than what is generally regarded as "normal." Gradually, they will rise to standing, develop a wide base of support and walk with a side-to-side, torso-shifting gait. Just as Torso-Sway Walker children are firmly rooted over their feet, so they are firmly rooted in their feelings and opinions. They will have struggled hard to reach a standing position and will need to affirm their independent stability.

This child will naturally stand with the weight of the body planted over widely spread feet.

Torso-Sway Walker children tend to be set in their ways. You might find that they have their own way of doing things and want others to understand their ideas in order to welcome them into their world. Torso-Sway Walker children will also probably be interested in a variety of things.

Look to find these children going into a profession that promises steadfastness and security. These children are at their best where they know the overall terrain well. They may become an agent, a systems designer, an advisor or a specialist of some sort.

If feeling insecure, they will hold their ground. It was hard-won, and they will not easily give up what they have accomplished.

While growing up, they may seem almost defiant in their apparent disinterest in what you have to say. These children are more interested in their own interpretation of the discussion at hand. One might say they can be "mono-focused"—or simply stubborn!

What Is the Best Way to Relate With Your Torso-Sway Walker Child?

These children should be encouraged to play, jump, take chances and learn to establish trust. It is critical that you as a parent let the Torso-Sway Walker child know that you will always be there for them. Though nurturing is of utmost importance to all children, a Torso-Sway Walker child needs special attention when it comes to trust and protection. Teach them to laugh at their own stubbornness.

In a supportive manner, let Torso-Sway Walker children know their uniqueness is celebrated, just as all of our uniqueness is celebrated. Even more important, they should be reassured that a tumble to the ground is only that, and that a first attempt is just a first attempt, not a failure.

Relations between Parents and Children

By now, you know what your own Bio-Type is as well as that of your child. What do you do with this information?

The great thing about realizing there are different Bio-Types is that it also helps to accept differences that may exist between you and your child. Understanding the different Bio-Types helps you work in a positive manner with your child, rather than getting frustrated because he doesn't understand why someone did something he would never have done himself. It takes the "right" and the "wrong" out of the equation. Let him learn sooner rather than later that different people are simply just that: Different.

Using what you know about your own Bio-Type can help you to relate with your children from the first crucial steps of their life. It helps you know how to better communicate with them and build a stronger relationship. Do not worry if they are already in 10th grade or finishing college! Your role as a guide lasts a lifetime.

By observing your child as he crawls, you are beginning to appreciate his way of perceiving things. You are starting to see the world from his point of view. The child's psychological relationship to everything that he encounters may be very different from your own. As a result, you can alter your interactions to consider these differences and even learn to look at your world from your child's perspective.

If You Are a Forward Faller

As a Forward Faller, you may find you have a tendency to look at the results you want to create as a parent—how you would like your child to see and do things—instead of how your child sees and appreciates things. You may find you secretly want to try controlling your child, forcing them into a mold, rather than allowing them the freedom to find a path of their own.

Try taking a step back, and watch how your child perceives things naturally on his own.

You, yourself, were watched and nurtured as a child. You felt secure in adventuring out into the world. Because of this, you may tend to be relatively fearless in your approach to new things. Do not be upset if your child is different.

You are also quick to go from the analytical to the emotional. These jumps might be natural to you but jarring to your child. Perhaps you find yourself becoming impatient with your child because he seems to be too slow to make shifts in his thoughts and emotions.

The great thing about realizing there are different Bio-Types is that we can begin to accept these differences in perception and methods of problem-solving to work with them rather than against them. We need to able to understand why others do not see the world the same way we do and honor their way of perceiving and doing things.

If You Are a Backward Faller

You are a person who got to your feet independently of any external support, and you expect others to do so as well. You have always been very independent and may tend to expect this same independence in your child. Enjoy the child you have. You are an excellent natural observer and, in fact, love to just watch and see what will happen in any given situation. Consequently, you might expect a similar nature from your little one.

You will probably see things that other parents miss and will want to help other parents see their own children more effectively. Other parents may even ask you to tell them what you can see about their children when they crawl and walk.

With your own child, you will be able to help him see things in a different light as well. Try not to suppress your child's naturally curious or impulsive nature by telling her repeatedly she will fall if she climbs too high. Better to provide quiet support by spotting in case she does slip, and observe instead your child's uncanny ability to balance. Let her show you who she is and what she can do. Try not to get upset if your child does not share your passion for observation or is too busy charging ahead to look at the world in the same way you do.

If You Are a Torso-Sway Walker

As a Torso-Sway Walker, if you think carefully about it, you may find that in your own childhood, you felt challenged in some way by the world around you. Therefore, you developed your own firm base of support in the way you stand and walk, with your feet slightly separated, supporting you in your firm stance. Remember that you probably have firm opinions. You may have felt challenged, and having overcome your challenges, you may unconsciously expect your child to overcome every challenge by standing fast or taking a stand too.

Be careful to let your child develop his own opinions about the world, especially if you find his opinions to be dramatically different from your own. Remember it does not need to be your way that he must follow; seek instead to become involved and fascinated by his way. You might tend to be an anchor around which he naturally moves, try finding a creative ways to let him be the anchor and to move yourself around his center.

As we grow with our children, we cheer and champion them as they begin to experiment with their physical movement. Children's natural curiosity will inspire them to explore how different parts of their bodies are connected when they find themselves moving around. Celebrate their physical discoveries with them! Set aside time to have fun, providing your child the opportunity to engage with their newly found physical selves. You get to have fun and connect with your child while helping your child develop motor skills, confidence, hand-eye coordination and brainpower. As a child's motor skills and thinking skills develop, they will want more independence. Partner with your child, inviting the child to participate in simple, daily life tasks. Be flexible, engaging, nurturing, and encouraging. Remember, no matter which Bio-Type, and how fast they grow up, while the child is in the developmental stages, always provide comfort when your little independent grownup, wants to be "just a kid" again.

11

Opening Doors

This book contains a simple—yet all-encompassing—way to open doors of understanding among individuals of very different temperaments. This book also offers easy-to-use tools to improve your interactions with the people that are important to you.

The concept is simple. Unlike other methods of personality typing that require asking of hundreds of questions and the subsequent analysis of the person's answers, the Bio-Typing method assumes that by the time you have asked questions, it is already too late. You never get a second chance to make a good first impression.

The reading of another person happens as you first observe and approach him. Bio-Typing is all about this initial observation, and Bio-Typing offers immediately applicable suggestions about approaching other people. You can know so much about another person at first glance—especially if it is a well-informed look. With the information in this book, you have the specifics to look at in that crucial first glance.

The simple "one-test" method of discerning Bio-Type is usually enough to know which personality type any individual falls into. Just in the same way that for some people, knowing another person's astrological sign may provide valuable information about him, Bio-Typing can give you specific, valuable information. However, where astrology is interpretive and subjective, Bio-Typing is looking at actual physical evidence of the other person's history, written in the movements of his body. Bio-Typing gives practical information on how to frame what you want to do and say to establish that connection you are seeking to make.

We often receive initial impressions of people, and then we disregard them because we unfortunately cannot substantiate these impressions. This book offers you both a way of substantiating what you see, and a practical guide to interacting with people you encounter, what I call "rules of engagement." The age, gender and social position of a person can make us lose sight of the child that he was when he shaped the body he lives in today, who he still is today. Bio-Typing teaches you to assess what he wants you to see, with what his body cannot hide about himself. In the end, most of us truly do want to be seen for who we really are.

Remember that I suggested that you try looking at yourself first, if you have not already done so. In doing so, you may well see both how accurate this system is and how differently various people see themselves in relation to their world and each other.

Applying what I have shown you in this book to your most significant relationships will make these relationships deeper and stronger. If you are like me, you may sometimes find yourself upset by the differences between your loved ones' interactions with the world and your own. Bio-Typing is a practical guide to opening your consciousness widely enough to include and embrace your loved ones' way of seeing and interacting with you and the world. Remember, embracing our differences makes embracing our loved ones more fulfilling!

Using this method in social and business interactions can make it easier to get what you want out of life. Embracing the differences in points of view and approaches to things can make the work you do with others more profitable—and enjoyable—to all.

In business, applying this new technology might allow you to know in advance how best to deal with a business associate to put him at ease or throw him off. You might find yourself going in the meeting thinking, "This person is a Backward Faller, so he will wait to hear what I have to say first before he tells me his idea."

Using the Bio-Typing "rules of engagement," you will not get off to a bad start by doing something that will put off a business associate. Instead, you will know how to best create accord with him before you start a business meeting. If the person with whom you hope to do business is a Torso-Sway Walker, you will know to give him the opportunity to tell you where he is coming from and how he sees himself and his company before you decide how best to use some part of what he says as a hook upon which to hang your presentation.

All too often, business is perceived as "beating" the opponent. Learning to survive through a deeper appreciation of human differences has taught me that harmony is always more profitable than merely surviving conflict. If you apply the recognition of personality differences and the "rules of engagement" I have developed in my own life to yours, you can only become more efficient and more appreciated by others. The less effort people need to make to understand you, the better they will like you. Even if they already like our ideas, effortless interaction is always beneficial.

A business associate doesn't need to accept your way of seeing and approaching things to find mutual benefit in your ideas, but intractability in your approach will undoubtedly turn him or her off before you get your idea across. At that point, it will not matter what could have been if only they had listened to you in the first place.

If you can achieve a deeper appreciation of the varied ways we all use in approaching and dealing with situations, you can shift your presentation to match your audience's way of absorbing information, thereby creating success for yourself in business.

If you see someone you would like to approach in a social situation, you might realize that he is a particular Bio-Type, and you are going to know how not to put him off when you approach him. If the individual is a Forward Faller, coming up with an exciting plan for an evening together may well get him interested, and he will let himself discover more about you as the evening progresses.

It has been very valuable for me to know that my wife is a Backward Faller and that when we have communication difficulties, she is going to look at things in a sequential way and weigh each aspect of a situation to come up with a methodical plan of action. As a Forward Faller, I will see only what I want to accomplish and just go for it, figuring out the steps along the way as I get to them. Then we might argue. She will argue fact-by-fact and I will say, "No, look at the big picture." Using the method in this book, I know how to talk to her in a more ordered fashion, approaching my goal in a way similar to how she would. She also knows how to talk to me, acknowledging my goals, so we can communicate better.

At home, if you create openness, awareness and acceptance of diversity in parent-child relations, your children will feel appreciated in their individuality and special in their uniqueness. The nurturing environment establishes a healthy, inclusive appreciation of you, the parent, and this naturally extends outside of the family into your children's world. Nothing makes us feel more secure than realizing that others see our world in ways similar to our own. But if we assume that how we see things is the "right" way or that there are no other ways of seeing oneself, the world becomes limited.

Where one child will be all about getting somewhere new and different, you can help that child really look at all the things around him right now. Alternatively, if the child is tentative and logical, you can open him with games of risk and adventure that stimulate other parts of the child's personality. If the child is wary, fearful and untrusting, you can create a setting that provides what he needs to feel nurtured and safe.

In the company of adults, the child is often the one at a disadvantage in reaching out to others. At first, this does not matter, because the child is the center of attention. Nevertheless, later on, when the child begins to feel the need to compete for attention among other children, an appreciation for the different ways of others takes on great importance. Where one child learns to become more demanding, the child who has learned differentiation in ways of reaching outward will find ways to get attention from others while giving attention to the individuals to whom he is reaching out.

Socially, children today face stiff competition early in life. If they appreciate early on, that each of us is unique and that these differences require different strategies for successful interaction, they will develop them.

In parent-child relationships, observing the way your child climbs to his feet will enable you to know a lot about how your child sees his world. By knowing where the child is coming from, you are going to be able to relate better to him and increase understanding between you. Your knowledge of your child's Bio-Type also offers you the opportunity to use games and toys with your child to develop other aspects of his physical and mental relationship with his own body. This will increase his physical capabilities and ways in which his mind develops, literally expanding his mind in earliest childhood and helping to develop areas that normally might otherwise go undeveloped.

My life has taught me that awareness of the differences among people is the starting place for all success in interacting with others. I sincerely hope sharing of what has worked for me will work just as well for you.

APPENDIX A

My Life Today

God gives in equal measure to each and every one of his children. Even if all the doors and windows of a child's body-temple remain forever locked, this house was never empty. God does not make garbage.

I am in my fifties, happily married and interacting pretty well with the people that used to seem so strange to me earlier in my life. In fact, I am working every day with people at my own studio. I do a type of life coaching, showing people how they use their bodies for as a paradigm for how they run their lives.

I also teach new physical problem-solving methodologies to make their lives more efficient.

For a lifetime, I have used my Bio-Typing method of looking at people in order to find a way to reach past the blindness to minds and faces that I was born with. Bio-Typing has allowed me to establish rules for myself to use in interacting with other people.

I have also used this understanding of people's bodies to help other people develop parts of their bodies they had never used. In doing so, they discover ways to do things differently in a physical sense. We have discovered that once the body starts to do things differently physically; the mind begins to approach and solve problems differently as well.

For example, since Backward Fallers always stands with their weight back over the heels, teaching them to bring their weight forward over the balls of the feet as a Forward Faller does make a Backward Faller more ready to step into new experiences. Or showing a Forward Faller how to find and use the muscles that spread the ribcage laterally, as a Torso-Sway Walker does, increases the Forward Faller's available lung capacity and helps him to breathe more deeply, which allows him greater stability.

I teach each of the three Bio-Types the best of what the other two do, in order to increase the overall functional efficiency of each one's own body.

Change the way you do things physically, and you profoundly change the way you do things in every other area of your life. Over the last 20 years, my clients have discovered that by learning how not to hurl themselves through a sit-up they also learn how not to hurl themselves through a relationship crisis. By learning to have and embrace physical balance, they have discovered emotional balance in other areas of their lives.

Change the way it feels to live in your body, and you change not only the way others see you but also the way in which you relate to yourself and all the other people in your life.

The great part of my work with people's bodies is that the changes in how they use their bodies seem to cause major changes in not only physical problem solving, but also in how they approach and solve problems in every arena of their lives. I guess this should not be too surprising, because after all, the models we use physically to perform any given action are the same ones our minds and hearts use in problem-solving elsewhere in life.

You can use this new way of looking at people to create advantages and opportunities for yourself in all your interactions with others.

I am currently teaching at Ryokan College of Psychology in Los Angeles, instructing future psychotherapists to see other people the way that I do. Others are appreciating me for figuring out how to survive and prosper given the deficits with which I was born. After a lifetime of struggling to get along and be understood by neurotypicals, they are letting me teach them what I have learned in order to interact with them. I feel so honored. God gives in equal measure to each of His children. What is truly a gift may not appear to be so at first glance. God does not make garbage.

APPENDIX B

Understanding Autism

Autism is diagnosed as a pervasive developmental disorder. It typically becomes apparent during the first three years of life. One parent describes how discovering his child's autism was as if someone had come in the night, stolen his child's personality and left a blank body. The child that remained was silent and sealed off in his own closed world. This is sometimes the way it happens, but not always.

Liane Holliday-Willey, in her book *Pretending to Be Normal: Living With Asperger's Syndrome*, says, "The autism umbrella is vast. Within its boundaries is a wide range of abilities and disabilities. It is a fluid diagnosis; one that has no definite beginning and no certain end. Scientists are uncertain as to how it is caused. Educators debate how to manage it. Psychologists are baffled about how to differentiate among its various labels. Parents are not certain how to deal with it. And those with autism are too often without any voice at all. Autism touches many, and yet, it is one of the most misunderstood developmental disorders."

Autism is the result of a neurological disorder that affects the functioning of the brain. The condition is to occur in as many as one in every 500 children. It is four times more prevalent in boys than in girls.

Autism seems to affect the development of the brain. People with autism typically have difficulties in the area of communication, social interactions and play activities. Autism makes it difficult for people to communicate and to relate to the outside world.

People with autism often exhibit repeated body movements such as rocking. Just as I have since childhood, I rock myself to sleep each night. Rocking helps me to process all of the jagged parts of the day's experiences and to re-find my center. We people with autism frequently are also either hypo- or hypersensitive to physical sensations. I typically wear really tight belts, and I sleep under a weighted blanket. These things give me a sense of safety.

People with autism also have resistance to changes in their routines. In other words, we like things to be the same all of the time. For example, I could happily eat pasta every single day. Individuals with autism may also experience perceptions differently from others. Sights, sounds and textures that neurotypicals easily process can cause great anxiety to someone with autism. I absolutely cannot tolerate the feel of peach skin. We often experience unusual things in the realm of the senses. In my case, I have frequent olfactory hallucinations. This means I smell things that are not there. I also sometimes cannot smell things that are there.

I tend to walk around things for no reason that would make sense to just about anyone else. Sometimes I can explain the things that bother me. At other times, I am at a complete loss for words. For example, I cannot walk across ropes in the sand that are set out for the volleyball courts on the beach. I cannot bear the sight of rubber gloves.

Did you know that a high concentration of people with Asperger's Syndrome and autism is found in Silicon Valley? It is because designing computer programs and the type of obsessively focused tasks involved in this industry are activities closely associated with the special talents of the minds of autistic people. We are naturally adept at seeing an extremely complex system clearly and being able to take in all of its parts and easily imagine how they all work together. I can easily imagine all of the 206 bones and more than 600 skeletal muscles that move a person's body. For the average person, this would be daunting to imagine all at once. The good news is that you do not need to. I have done it for you. You just need to look at specific parts of the body doing specific actions to benefit from what I discovered.

More than a half-million people in the U.S. today have autism. Its prevalence rate makes autism one of the most common of developmental disabilities. Yet most of the public, including many professionals in the medical, educational, and vocational fields, are still unaware of how autism affects people and how to work effectively with individuals with autism.

In the dinosaur days, when autism was considered the result of having a "refrigerator mother," a cold and uninvolved parent, my own mother was infinitely patient with me, ever seeking to understand why I did the things I did and making me feel special and important. She would often tell me that if I wanted to do something others might find unusual or weird, it was OK, that it was good, because God did not create me capable of wanting things that were bad. She would then point out a more successful way of achieving the sensation or thing I wanted.

The actions of others are often confusing to people with autism, and we may withdraw from social interactions. Many of us have difficulty with interactive play. This might have something to do with why I cannot abide things and places that remind me of my abysmal failures at sports.

We may have difficulty picking up social clues, so our actions may not be appropriate to the situation. We may find human contact stressful at times or show an unusual focus in our sensory experiences, such as an exaggerated interest in smell or in repetitive, rhythmic motion.

We also do something called "perseverating." This means we get like a dog on a bone about issues that are important to us. I can talk anyone's ears off about certain subjects, such as atypical muscle innervation patterns or the way governments should be managed.

There are also many myths and misconceptions about autism. Contrary to popular belief, many people with autism do make eye contact; it just may be less or different from the way others do it. If I am explaining something that requires my full attention to get it right, I will often stare at your shoe (or whatever), so I am not distracted from my train of thought and forming a sequence of words to express it.

At a conference in Michigan, I was once performing a mime show about what the world of autism feels like from the inside. A United States senator who had worked long and hard to get Congress to provide autism funding for his state was at a special dinner at the conference. To Liane and my wife's horror, I walked over to the senator and began talking to him about coming to see my show the next night. Liane and my wife had no notion of what we were talking about; did I mention that I perseverate on my views of politics?

So there I am, on one knee, talking to this senator, and my wife and Liane are getting a little frantic because they are certain that I might be telling this man how to run the United States government. I was merely inviting him to see the mime show because I thought it could help him better understand his nephew, who has autism. When the senator asked me some questions, I naturally shifted my focus to his shoes in order to carefully, cohesively form my thoughts and respond.

Many people with autism can develop good functional communication skills. One significant insight I got from a very special woman who works with autistic children is that I have to translate the words spoken to me into pictures in order to understand them. Then I translate my thoughts and feelings back into words in order to respond.

Often I will know or understand things but will not be able to express them in words unless I make a concerted effort. I will stare off into the distance for a bit and then tune back in. Once I have found the words to express a thought or feeling, I can repeat that sequence of words whenever I need to express or explain the thing I have understood.

Children born with autism do not "outgrow" autism, but many of the symptoms can lessen as the child develops. I have not banged my head against anything for quite a while now.

One of the most devastating myths about people with autism is that some people actually believe we cannot feel or show affection. This is patently ridiculous! We feel too much! We often have trouble finding the words to say what we feel. My students will tell you that I often get extremely emotional and teary-eyed over a word or a thought; I just also clam up and cannot explain why my eyes are leaking.

I wrote this poem after talking to a therapist who worked with children with autism. She had been explaining to me that children who banged their heads did not feel anything anyway, so head banging was reflex-action. As a head banger, I got somewhat upset but could not explain it to her right away. So I wrote—

I once heard that God does not make garbage

Why do you study me from a distance and through a glass?
Why do you speak about me behind my back?
And why do you whisper when you talk about me?

Other parents talk on and on, loudly and proudly, about each new little thing that their child does.

Why do you whisper and glance around furtively?
Do you fear that someone might think that you created me, not God?
That the me that you created will reflect inadequacies in you.
That society might reject you because of me?

I once heard that God does not make garbage,
then who made me?

Am I a disease that you might catch?

Are my idiosyncrasies little germs that might infect you and make those parts that are
different in you begin to grow?

Believe it or not, I am a human being too, just like you.
My need for love and understanding is just
wrapped up in different colored paper.

If looking into your eyes makes me forget all the things I need to say, this doesn't mean
I'm stupid, or in another world or not present.
It's just that your eyes are so deep and so filled with so many things that they, your eyes,
can confuse me.
I can too easily get lost among all the fascinating things I see.

Sometimes, if I don't respond it's not cause I'm too stupid to understand English.
It's that words are so slippery at times and the same words can mean so many different
things.
And other times, I simply can't easily grab onto and use the words you might under-
stand to say "thank you" or "I love you."
But it doesn't mean I have no feelings.
I have too many.

I have heard that people only really fear the things that attract them.
The tall building draws and repels the man afraid of heights.
Could you be drawn to my uniqueness cause it resonates with some unexplored part of
you?

The ancients used to metaphorically pile their sins onto the back of a goat and then
drive the poor animal out into the desert to die of starvation.
Am I the scapegoat that must be driven away in order to expiate parts of normal peo-
ple that must never be explored?

Do you fear that your membership in society might be revoked if you ever admitted that you might be just a little like me?

Maybe my peculiarities are really, just reflections of the things in you that you are afraid to look too closely at.

And why are you so embarrassed by my honesty, so ashamed of my uniqueness?
Will too much fascination with one thing diminish you?
Might it not open doors of discovery for all mankind
(your kind and my kind)

Forget my little tics and my strange little rituals for just a second and weigh my honesty and my loyalty against artificial facades and hidden meanings.

If God does not make garbage, then who made me?

Maybe I am a gift that you just forgot to open!

© Johnny Seitz

APPENDIX C

About Johnny Seitz

By Dr. Adam Sheck, Psy. D.

Johnny Seitz is an innovator. His book offers an opportunity to its readers to know themselves at an incredibly deep new level. How can I describe Johnny Seitz? I can talk about Johnny Seitz, the human being. I can tell you about Johnny Seitz, my friend. I can tell you about Johnny Seitz, the man with the "label" of autism. I could tell you how he ingeniously developed a way of interacting with the world that is nothing short of miraculous.

Actually, I could fill a book talking about Johnny; he's that rich and fascinating a man. However, my purpose here is to speak about Johnny Seitz, the author, and I'll keep it short and to the point. This book is his gift to "neurotypicals," those people with "normal" mental wiring, the majority of people in our world. It is a gift that can allow you to live a richer, fuller life.

Growing up in the world of autism, Johnny was severely challenged in attempting to relate to what he senses as "emotional mind-fields." Intuitively, as a survival mechanism, Johnny learned to "read" people from the outside in. He focused on their physical body language, on their "human biomechanics." The body doesn't lie, and so he found an authentic way to connect with others, a way which to appears to many to mirror the magic of the mind reader and the psychic. Johnny synthesizes the information provided by human biomechanics into a language of its own, which he calls Bio-Typing.

Speaking as a clinical psychologist, I know there is a deep connection between the mind and the body. This is nothing new. The work of psychologists and psychotherapists is supporting each patient in connecting to himself and to his psyche, so he can gain the freedom to express himself more fully in life. Most psychotherapy is "talk therapy," where psychotherapist and patient sit and commune primarily through the medium of speaking and listening. There also exist a number of "somatic psychotherapies," which work more directly with the human body.

In my personal and professional experience, Johnny's Bio-Typing work goes deeper than any of these psychotherapies. In this book, Johnny provides us with the three basic Bio-Types that we all fit into. Knowing about these Bio-Types provides us with the most basic, straightforward information regarding people's orientation to their world. This is the foundation of Johnny's "magic."

And now, this magic is yours. Many secrets lie in this book. Using them, you can understand yourself and others to a degree you never imagined possible. Your world will expand with the language of Bio-Typing. This information, this new perspective can change your life. It will change your life if you choose to apply it.

Bibliography

Bowlby, J. 1980. *Attachment and Loss: Loss, Sadness and Depression.* Hogarth Press. London

Dychtwald, K. 1986. *Bodymind.* Penguin Putnam Inc. New York

Grandin, T. 1995. *Thinking in Pictures.* Vintage Books. New York

Holliday Willey, L. 1999. *Pretending to be Normal.* Jessica Kingsley Publishers. London

Holliday Willey, L. 2001 *Asperger's Syndrome in the Family: Redefining Normal* Jessica Kingsley Publishers. London.

Holliday Willey, L., ed. 2003 *Asperger's Syndrome in Adolescence: Living With the Ups, the Downs and Things in Between.* Jessica Kingsley Publishers. London.

Kurtz, R. and Presera M.D., H. 1984. *The Body Reveals.* Harper Collins. New York

Maurice, C. 1993. *Let Me Hear Your Voice.* Ballantine Books. New York

Morris, D. 1977. *Manwatching A Field Guide To Human Behavior.* Harry N. Abrams Inc., Publishers. New York

Ornstein, Ph. D., R. 1993. *Roots of the Self.* Harper Collins. New York

Reber, A; Reber, E., Reber E.S. 2001. *Penguin Dictionary of Psychology* (3d ed) Penguin. New York

Zilberter, M.D.,T. 2004 *'Brain Hemispheres'* www.dietandbody.com/article1164.html

Suggested Further Reading

http://www.autism-society.org/autism.html, on autism

http://www.neuroacoustic.com/articlesleeptext.htm, on Beta, Alpha, Theta and Delta brainwaves

http://www.tonyattwood.com/paper4.htm, on Asperger's Syndrome

About the Book

Bio-Typing: Beyond Body-Language is about assessing and understanding ourselves, as well as other people. It is written by a unique individual who desperately needed a method in order to physically identify people and understand how to deal with social relationships. Johnny Seitz is an adult with autism. He developed Bio-Typing as an exceptional coping skill.

With autism, Johnny Seitz lives in a very different place than most of us "normal people" (neurotypicals). Normal people are able to look at each other's faces and determine identity, mood and intention. Johnny Seitz cannot. He is "mind-blind". He has taught himself to see and quantify subtle patterns indicators in another's movements, which profile the individual with amazing accuracy. And yet, Johnny Seitz's Bio-Typing inspires genuine curiosity about human connections; his method is so easily learned and ultimately is applicable in our everyday life from the most mundane to the most excruciating arenas.

Bio-Typing will lead you through the author's personal journey of understanding and the process he deftly passes on to you, enhancing your own understanding of yourself and the people in your world. This book will take you back to the child you were so long ago. It will create in you an awakening into the world you inhabit today and show you a side of the spectrum we call life, as you never imagined it to be. It will enable you to understand the adult you have become and give you the tools to step forward and transform. This is the roadmap of the human psyche written across our bodies. This is the fruit of an impassioned lifetime. Come, sit down, and partake.

About the Author

Johnny Seitz is an internationally recognized mime, personal life-coach, professional ballet dancer, choreographer and an adult with autism. He has made astonishing new discoveries about the bodies we inhabit and the parallel relationship between the patterns in our bodies and those of our minds. Johnny has taught at Harvard, NYU and Princeton, as well as privately throughout Europe and the Americas. Johnny Seitz currently maintains a private practice and lives in Los Angeles and is on the faculty of Ryokan College of Psychology.

0-595-31677-8

www.ingramcontent.com/pod-product-compliance
Lightning Source LLC
Chambersburg PA
CBHW031320290526
45784CB00014B/416